CN00735417

"Brilliant and delicious chips for the soul. Eat just one a day? No way. I can't stop. Great tiny tales, tips, and thoughts."

Derek Sivers, author, *How to Live*

"An inspiring, heart-warming, go-getting book. *365 Ways to Have a Good Day* is an antidote to apathy and the kickstart we all need to live our best life."

Helen Tupper, co-author of *The Squiggly Career*

"Equal parts funny and touching and yet in all ways wise, *365 Ways to Have a Good Day* is more than a path to having better days; it's a simple, compelling structure to support the daily art and practice of living a better life."

Jerry Colonna, author, *Reboot: Leadership and the Art of Growing Up*

"This book is a user manual for the next 24 hours. And the rest of your life. Our lives are decided by our daily practice. The problem is that most daily practices are done once a week, once a month, and for some, only once a year. Hmmm. But if you stop trying to change your life and lower the bar a little, and focus only on today. That's right, just the next 24 hours. And repeat that. Gradually, then suddenly, you will be living your best life. Because days change weeks. Months change years. Years change decades. Decades change lives."

David Hieatt, cofounder, The Do Lectures

"It is always a good day when you get to tap into Ian's wisdom and with *365 Ways to Have a Good Day* you get a dose of Ian's reflective optimism, daily. *365 Ways* is your guide to reclaiming how you choose to approach each and every day. It's a daily invitation to look at what's before you from a novel or different angle. Ian's advice will both challenge AND energize your usual routine – which is a rather perfect way to proceed to have a good day if you ask me!"

J. Kelly Hoey, author, *Build Your Dream Network*

"Innovative thinker and life designer Ian Sanders expands our minds again in his new book *365 Ways to Have a Good Day!* We'd all like to find the magical gateway to everyday happiness, the truth is, life ebbs and flows. Ian gives us a tactical roadmap to hack our brains so that we can experience a state of joy more often than not, even on the bad days."

Espree Devora, tech founder and podcaster

365 WAYS TO HAVE A GOOD DAY

365 WAYS
TO HAVE A GOOD DAY

BY IAN SANDERS

First published in Great Britain by John Murray Learning in 2021
An imprint of John Murray Press
A division of Hodder & Stoughton Ltd,
An Hachette UK company

1

A CIP catalogue record for this title is available from the British Library

Hardback ISBN 9781529382242
eBook ISBN 9781529382266

Typeset by KnowledgeWorks Global Ltd.

Printed and bound in Great Britain by Clays Ltd, Elcograf S.p.A.

John Murray Press policy is to use papers that are natural, renewable and recyclable products and made from wood grown in sustainable forests. The logging and manufacturing processes are expected to conform to the environmental regulations of the country of origin.

John Murray Press
Carmelite House
50 Victoria Embankment
London EC4Y 0DZ

www.johnmurraypress.co.uk

To Zoë, Barney and Dylan – thanks for all the good days
xxx

CONTENTS

ABOUT THE AUTHOR

Photograph by Paul Tait

Ian Sanders has built an unconventional career out of following his curiosity and sharing what he's learned along the way.

This journey of discovery has opened all kinds of unexpected doors including working for BBC local radio while still a teenager; launching a marketing business by accident and running ad campaigns for Benetton; writing about work and business for the *Financial Times*; training BBC journalists about storytelling; working backstage for the digital media team at The World Economic Forum in Davos; giving talks at various events including South By South West Interactive in Austin, Texas and The Do Lectures; running workshops for organizations such as General Assembly, Ericsson and Microsoft; leading urban-walk coaching sessions; being managing director of a radio studio business; and co-managing a band.

Throughout his professional life, Ian has experimented with life-enhancing habits and hacks. It's resulted in two decades' worth of conversations, detours and journals. A self-confessed 'work-in-progress' Ian's always been open about his own struggles and difficult days, and his decision to build more good ones. And now, whether it's working with teams in global organizations or with a founder who's just getting started, Ian aims to spark change. With 365 Ways to Have a Good Day, he hopes to inspire people to spark change in their own lives, and to get more out of every day.

Ian lives in Leigh-on-Sea with his wife, two teenage sons and their border terrier and can often be found swimming in the sea. This is his fifth book.

INTRODUCTION

I'd just finished giving a presentation at a company's awayday in the foothills of the Bavarian Alps. There was an hour to kill before the car would come to take me to Munich Airport. I had a choice how to fill my time: either to catch up on emails in the hotel or go and find the lake at the bottom of the hill.

I chose the latter. The woman behind the reception desk handed me a map, a towel and a key to the hotel's *Badeplatz*. Once there, I knew I'd made the right choice. It was stunning: just me by myself, swimming in this perfectly still lake with a view of the mountains ahead, clear blue skies above.

This experience crystallized my thoughts that day, symbolizing something so true – you can live your life straightjacketed by what you *think* you should do, or you can choose to live your best life. A life that energizes and fulfils you. A life that's aligned with your passions, spirit and values. That's what I was doing that Tuesday morning as I swam in that German lake.

I've worked for myself for over two decades. I've had highs and lows. I've suffered burnout. There have even been times when I've thought about giving up the independent way of life. But there's a guiding philosophy at the core of how I live. It became clear to me the time I returned home from a year-end meeting with my accountant, during which we'd reviewed a disappointing 12 months. Afterwards, somewhat deflated, I talked to my wife Zoë. She pointed out something I'd said about those 12 months – that although they might have been less than financially rewarding, they'd been some of the happiest of my life. It crystallised to me then that my version of success isn't pinned on traditional notions of money and status.

I'm a work-in-progress on myself. Tuning in to what really matters. Shaping my philosophy, which is now as much a part of me as breathing: **this is my life not a business model.**

It's not my goal to squeeze productivity and money out of every waking minute. I'd rather live the best life I can. And at the heart of that desire is knowing what a good day looks like and aiming to have more of them!

Having a good day affects your happiness, creativity, productivity and wellbeing. It makes a difference not just to yourself, but to your partner, family, friends and colleagues.

So for the last ten years, I've been on an active journey of exploration and discovery to see what I could learn. A decade of journalling, experimenting with behaviours, working with teams in organizations, mentoring others, and conversations with experts and people in my network – everything I've uncovered has gone into this book.

This guide includes stories to inspire you, prompts to put ideas into action and tips to try out. When you know what's right for you, you'll do more of it, and that will help you become more productive, creative, fulfilled and happier.

For me, I'll always take the lake over the emails. I only have one life after all – I'd rather live the best one I can.

I'm delighted you're joining me on my quest to have more good days.

Ian Sanders, May 2021

hello@iansanders.com

iansanders.com

CHAPTER 1
DESIGN YOUR OWN OPERATING SYSTEM

1   Think like a chef

A good day is not something that's set in stone.

It's going to change. As you change.

So think like a chef. Experiment in your kitchen, grab ingredients and throw them in the pot. Taste and add seasoning. Before serving up a tasty and healthy 'good day' dish.

Try things. See what works. Play with the suggestions in this book and discover what brings you results or just makes you feel better.

We all have our unique ways of operating in the world. What I identify as a good day won't necessarily be the same for you.

It's up to you to decide those ingredients you'd like to flavour your life.

2   Design your own operating system

The words 'operating system' – what do they make you think of? Perhaps the software that runs your phone or computer.

But actually each of us has our own unique operating system.

What's mine? It's knowing what matters most to me. And then living my life true to that.

These are the key components inside my operating system: freedom, independence, doing things my way, making time during the working day for daily walks or summer swims, sitting in coffee shops, moving around, not being shackled to a desk, working with people who stimulate and energize me, being curious and creative, trying new things, always moving forward.

My system is built on the working habits and behaviours that fuel my best work.

Identify the habits, behaviours and mindsets that are right for you. Nail them down. Hard-bake them into your life. This is your operating system. It'll run in the background, and enable you to function as your best You.

3   Track your Good Times

It's at the heart of making sure I have a good day.

The perfect 'app' for tracking those positive moments and experiences, so I have a clearer sense of who I am, what I stand for and what makes me tick. It's the ideal way to reflect on my life – both personal and professional – and check-in on how I'm doing.

This app doesn't require a subscription. All I need is a notepad and pen.

It's my Good Times list. A simple numbered list in my notepad. Each list runs Monday to Sunday.

Getting a round of applause at the end of a talk. A lazy Friday lunch with a friend. Walking through the autumnal leaves in Regent's Park.

In eight years of old notepads, my Good Times ritual has given me my best metric for success.

Give it a go.

Each day reflect on those thoughts, moments and experiences that make you feel most you. At the end of the week look back over the list. What patterns emerge? What do you need to do more of?

And keep it going.

4   Look for the positive

I don't call my journalling habit Bad Times. I call it Good Times.

Of course I have crappy moments in life, it's just that I don't keep a list of them.

That's why I believe my Good Times habit has changed my outlook. It's optimized me to scan everyday life for the positive. It's taught me the importance of living in the moment, of noticing and of appreciating what I've got, and guiding me to do more of it.

It's the one simple daily ritual that ensures I stay focused on what's important.

Every day, look out for the positive.

5   Notice your breathing

Michael Townsend Williams, the author of *Do Breathe*, and I were walking alongside the Thames when he pointed out one of those rather obvious things, that is only obvious once someone tells you about it. Namely, breathing is the only major system in the body that can be consciously as well as unconsciously controlled.

We have agency over how we breathe.

And therefore, Michael explains, we can use it to our advantage. As we walked, he suggested we slow down and notice our breathing.

Try it now.

Breathe in deeply through the nose. And out through the mouth. Do it three times.

Do you feel calmer now? More relaxed? More present in your body?

Michael explained that the simple act of breathing and noticing makes you aware of your current state. And also, it enables you to change it through the way you breathe.

Breathing slowly like that can lower your heart rate and dampen the impact of stress and anxiety.

6   Get your fingers tattooed!

Imagine if your younger self could take steps to make sure your older self wouldn't go off track.

That's Ian Rogers' story. In his early 20s Ian got a tattoo. It stretches across his right hand and onto his fingers.

Ian started his career building a website for the Beastie Boys while he was a teenager. He went on to work in senior roles at Apple Music and the luxury brand group LVMH. He's currently with French fintech startup Ledger.

He said it was as if his younger self was trying to protect his older self: that wherever he worked it wouldn't matter if he had tattoos on his fingers.

I love it. It's like his tattoo is a compass. It makes sure he chooses the right path in life.

What stamp can you put on your life to make sure you're on the right path?

7   Start your day well

How do you typically start your working day?

My formula for having a good start involves these three tried-and-tested habits:

1. Go for a walk on the beach.
2. Pick up a takeout coffee.

3. Start work with some upbeat tunes listening to Lauren Laverne's show on BBC 6 Music.

Daily habits matter. How you begin informs how your day pans out.

Groggily reaching for your phone on the bedside table, aimlessly scrolling? Or getting up early and heading out for a walk?

What do you need to get going strong? And can you set it up as a daily ritual?

8 Look inside your snow globe

There's a lovely guy I know who lives in Baltimore. His name is John Waire.

John is a talented photographer as well as having a gift with words.

On our calls we'll have a great chat and then he'll reflect back what I've said. It gets me reaching for my pad to scribble it down.

During the pandemic, he told me what he'd noticed now life had slowed down. Before it all happened, he likened our lives to busy snow globes, where we were always on the go, full of movement. A whirling chaos.

And then the pandemic hit and forced us to stop still for a while. Now, John said, the snow globes had settled. We could all see what really matters.

When you step out of the frenetic pace of life, you can let those snowflakes settle for a moment. When that happens you can look around and notice. Stop and take it in. What do you notice now that you just couldn't see before?

9   Recognize the simplicity of a perfect day

We drove 75 minutes to a remote stretch of coastline where our friend Dan has a little beach house on stilts.

Our relationship goes back to when we met at school at 11 years old. We know each other well. We are easy company. Dan's probably the only one of my friends where we don't discuss work or business.

It was great to hang out at a secluded, idyllic spot for a few hours. Nothing fancy, simply having our two families together, out on the terrace, off the grid in the middle of summer. We did uncomplicated things. Tucking into a cheese and tomato salad, sharing stories, going for a swim. Laughing. Not talking about work.

That was enough. That was enough for my 52nd year on my planet. Period.

Those simple ingredients – they magnified me.

10   Know what success looks like

I heard a podcast the other day where a startup founder asserted he'd be a success once he'd created wealth ten times what he's worth today. That's one view.

Here's another. Long ago Allan quit his own career as an entrepreneur to become a therapist. He loves what he does. It's not about the money. It's about helping others.

So how about you – what does 'success' mean to you?

In my early 20s my answer would have been ticking off my career goals, as well as status and money. Now, success is about living a life true to who I really am.

11   Tune in to yourself

When I was growing up in the 1970s we had a big chunky Roberts radio.

When I was unwell enough to be off school, my mum would bring the radio up to my bedroom. I loved scanning the frequency dials, twisting the heavy knob until I found something I wanted to listen to.

I liked that transformation where it went from fuzzy to crystal clear as you moved the dial.

And I think that's what we can all do in order to tune in to ourselves.

Take your vintage radio and tune into who you are. What are those experiences when you feel most You?

   Drinking coffee out of a ceramic cup.

   Sitting with a small glass of wine and reading the weekend newspaper.

   Taking photographs.

What will you hear when you have tuned out of the static and into You?

12   If you want to change your mindset, take a journey

A change in location can change your state of mind, so if you need to alter your mindset, try altering your scenery.

A journey is my best place for mind wandering, for scribbling ideas and for getting clarity.

Taking journeys to new places and walking along streets I've never trod before always energizes me. It provides fuel for me and my business, helping with new ideas or looking at things from a different perspective.

And it provides those essential moments of joy and aliveness.

There's something about travel which is so liberating, that freshens my thoughts. I love change and delight in the new, the different, the unfamiliar. I always return reinvigorated.

13 Zoom in on the little things

It's often the little things that can make a big difference to your day.

The first coffee of the day. Having the right stationery to hand. Leafing through a newspaper. A slice of homemade cake. Lighting a candle. Playing that track by The Chemical Brothers again.

So each day I'm zooming in to notice – and celebrate – these little things.

How about you? What are the little things you can zoom in on that make a difference to your day?

14 Find *arbejdsglæde*

I asked my friend Nick Creswell what it's like working for a Danish company. On a call from his apartment in Copenhagen, he explained there are many differences. There is an openness in communication, a lack of hierarchy. Healthy working conditions – a set amount of space between desks, a source of natural light – are not only encouraged, they are stipulated by law. And on your birthday, he said you'll find your desk festooned with Danish flags and have the chance to share delicious pastries with your colleagues.

Perhaps this is why the Danish have a word for happiness at work: *arbejdsglæde*.

What changes could you make in your job or office to find more joy at work?

15 Have good quality relationships

One of the most comprehensive long-term studies in history on happiness, the Harvard Study of Adult Development, has conducted research for 75 years. In his TEDx talk, the study's director Robert Waldinger outlines the findings on the key to a good life. Namely, it's the quality of your relationships.

It found that being socially connected is good for you, and loneliness has adverse effects. And then the quality of the relationship is important – warm relationships give us a sense of protection. Additionally, if in later life you have someone you can rely on – even if you bicker with your partner from time to time – it's good for your brain: you'll have better memories.

One more piece of advice from Robert: ditch the family feud, they can have a seriously detrimental effect on the grudge-holders.

16 Go outside the matrix

There are so many days I live 'in the matrix' of daily life, Bree Groff told me. And to have a good day she needs at least one moment outside of that.

Bree is a partner at SYPartners, the US transformation consulting firm, and lives in Tribeca, Manhattan.

She explains that so many days are packed with the usual ingredients of a busy executive who's also a parent of young children. A fast shower, making school lunch, meeting after meeting, remembering to make a dentist appointment, a bit of TV and sleep.

That's why she needs at least one moment out of the matrix.

It could be a few minutes being amused by the birds playing tag outside her apartment window. Or a phone call with her parents. Or the delight of adding a square of chocolate to her afternoon coffee.

Those moments remind her not only that life is short, but that the world is a beautiful place.

17 Tolerate the hard parts

On the first afternoon of our walking holiday in Yorkshire it wouldn't stop raining. As my wife, two sons and I climbed the hill the rain pelted down. It was hard to walk without slipping over. We got soaked. Wet ferns slapped against our legs. But we loved it!

We got to the top, and took in the magnificent scenery spread out before us. Our enthusiasm hadn't been dented by the weather.

That same holiday we stayed in the worst Airbnb I have ever experienced. Drawers were full of old junk, there was mould on the walls behind the tatty drapes, the carpet in the bathroom was greying and stained. I could go on but it makes me shiver to think about it. Ok, we'll bear it, we thought.

After too many nights there I was pleased to move to our next accommodation. We'd booked a cabin in a different spot for the last night. It was clean and modern. Mould free! We lay down on the clean bedding, breathed a sigh of relief and felt lifted.

So the question is: would those highs have been the same without the lows?

18 Find your *ikigai*

What gives you a spring in your step when you get out of bed in the morning?

If you're really fortunate it might be because you have found your *ikigai*.

Ikigai is a Japanese concept meaning 'a reason for being.'

On the island of Okinawa in Japan, the residents hold the record for being the longest living people on earth. It's partly thought that *ikigai* might be one of the reasons for this. Finding your *ikigai* can require a deep and often lengthy search of self which, ultimately, leads to a life that is worth living. It's about having meaning and purpose in life, where your wishes, requirements, aspirations and fulfilment all come together.

19   Get some lightbulbs in the shower

Where do you get your best ideas?

I've been asking that question for five years. And the most common answer I get is: in the shower.

If standing under a jet of water gets your ideas flowing, you have something in common with Hollywood screenwriter Aaron Sorkin, who found having a shower helps with writer's block. So much so he got a shower installed in his office. He reportedly used to take up to eight showers a day to keep those Oscar-award winning ideas flowing. Forget the quality of his work, just think about how clean he is!

So what's going to give you your best ideas? Know what it is and do more of it.

20   Always head towards You

In my first few weeks of university, I'd joined a bunch of fellow students on a night out to Leeds city centre. As I sat on the top deck of the number 655 bus that night, being cajoled into joining in with their banter and football songs, I became keenly aware: this wasn't my crowd.

I've thought of that uncomfortable experience over the years when I've felt a similar feeling, not just in social situations but professional ones too. I'm sure it's the same for many of us, when we've stuck at jobs that we dislike or experienced workplace cultures that are at odds with who we are and what we stand for.

At the 2012 Do Lectures – an experience totally aligned with who I am – Edward Espe Brown gave a talk about his experiences as a Zen priest. He told us how having sat still for 30,000 hours had made him very good at heading towards Edward.

On that night out in Leeds, I might have been heading into the city, but I certainly wasn't heading towards me. How about you? Are you good at heading towards You?

And be careful who you get on the bus with ;)

21   In a crisis, look for growth

For a few Fridays in April and May 2020, my wife and I tuned in, along with hundreds of others around the world, to 'This Human Moment'. It was a weekly online series live-streamed by Keith Yamashita from his home in California to help us through the crises we were experiencing: COVID-19 and ensuing economic fallout, plus the social upheaval triggered by the death of George Floyd.

This Human Moment was pinned on the idea that out of such difficulty we can strive for personal renewal and development, that we can experience 'post-traumatic growth'. Adversity can be a springboard to better things.

Keith was the perfect host. He's a business leader who suffered a devastating stroke at the age of 51. He's written of how it robbed him of the abilities he took for granted, being unable to work for seven months. But he realized that his stroke was a rare opportunity for renewal. Keith saw that there might possibly be a different kind of flourishing to be had on the other side.

So when challenged by a traumatic event or unexpected crisis, can we too look for post-traumatic growth and renewal?

22 Be who you needed when you were younger

Did you get the support, encouragement and inspiration you needed when you were growing up?

When I was at school it was my dream to work in radio and TV.

My headmaster told me to forget it.

But I decided to stick to my dream and got my lucky break when BBC local radio came to my town. I was off! I went on to have a 12-year career in broadcasting.

Ten years after walking out of the school gates I got asked to go back to give advice to students at a careers fair.

I decided to go and be who I needed when I was younger.

So when you get in a position to help, mentor and guide people starting out – be who you needed when you were younger. Deliver that guest lecture, go and give that talk to the school kids, provide an alternative perspective and counter the naysayers.

23 Know when you're at your peak

Whether you're an early bird or a night owl, the trick is to tune into when you're at your best and, where possible, adjust your schedule and behaviours accordingly.

My best time tends to be between 9 am and 11 am and I try to do the work that really matters – ideas, important calls – then.

For Claire Van der Zant – who's chief operating officer at a promotions company – it's earlier. Claire's most alive at 7am so it's then she does her creative and analytical work. She fades at 11am so finds that a good time for admin, whereas I tend to do mine in the afternoon.

And like most of us, she feels it's around 3pm when her energy levels are low, so that's when she'll take a break in order to get going again.

Of course you don't always get to choose – often you're scheduled tasks outside your control. But if you can pay attention to when you do your work, and can arrange your workload accordingly, it will make a huge difference to your productivity, output and mood.

24   Get some downtime

It sounds unproductive doesn't it?

'Downtime.'

Time that is down, out, on hold, unproductive. Like when your online banking is offline, or when the office coffee machine is broken.

Actually, downtime is a chance to explore and renew, so making space for it is essential. When I'm in an unfamiliar city to give a talk, I might give myself a half day to walk and wander, to sit and daydream. These are some of my favourite, and creatively productive, times.

In his book *In Praise of Wasting Time*, Alan Lightman says downtime enables not only your creativity, but also the formation and maintenance of your deep sense of being and identity. The freedom to ponder your past and imagine your future. And when you put it like that, it really is key.

25   Put You in your work

Nine years ago I shared a car journey from west Wales to Heathrow Airport with an artist and design teacher from New York City, James Victore. James said if you're ever in town, look me up.

The following year I rocked up at his Williamsburg studio. He explained that young designers often came to his studio to show him their work. They wanted his feedback. James told me their work mostly looked fine but there was always one thing missing.

Them! They don't put themselves in their work.

James says you should bring your unique qualities – your passions, your personality – to your work, otherwise you're just making something that's mediocre. He was speaking about designers, but that message struck me between the eyes. I shot a little video of him on my phone relating that story and, for a few years afterwards, I would play it to students when I was invited to guest lecture at universities.

As James subsequently wrote in his book, *Feck Perfuction*, let your love, fears and interests saturate your work. Who you are is the most important part of your work – never leave it out.

26   Work on your internal happiness

Having a good day starts with getting to know yourself, understanding what makes you tick and what you find enjoyable. My friend Emily Morris is a therapist. She says uncovering these elements can be very useful in guiding you on the choices you make in life.

Emily says that working on your internal happiness – being interested in yourself, knowing yourself, understanding why you feel the way you do – can lead to a more fulfilling and satisfying day than someone who invests all their time in pursuing an externally focused idea of a good day, such as seeking approval for looking good or appearing successful.

Today, think about the things you're doing. Are they for you, or other people? Are you enjoying them or do they make you feel depleted? Start tuning into what lifts you up and what you do to take yourself forward.

27 Find your own retreat

One hour drive from my house is one of the oldest churches in the UK. The Chapel of St Peter-on-the-Wall dates back to the year 660. It's on a beautiful, deserted stretch of coastline. The chapel is approached on foot, quite a stroll from the nearest village.

And it was here that I went on a mindfulness and yoga retreat.

There was only one problem – I'd never even done yoga. And while I wanted to give it a try – and I loved the idea of it – I found yoga wasn't really for me. So I made my apologies and went off by myself.

I remember that Sunday morning, just before 7am, sitting on the grass outside the ancient chapel.

Just looking out.

Stillness. Solitude. Birdsong and bees. The hum of a ship far out at sea. Wind in the trees. A rabbit darting in the grass.

It was like a raw experience of what it feels to be alive. A realization of life at its basic. I'd stumbled upon my own mindfulness retreat.

28 Smile at each other in the lift

There's a building I used to visit regularly. A company headquarters.

When I first got into a lift there, I was surprised.

I said hello to the people who joined me in the lift and they looked at me like I was mad! It felt like that scene in the film *Crocodile Dundee* where Paul Hogan's character – who's from the Australian outback and seeing a big city for the first time – says hello to strangers when he's walking down a Manhattan street.

Come on, this is your office lift not a tube carriage! I didn't even work there, but as a guest who was working in the building that day, I wanted to make an effort.

Let's smile and say hello to each other in the lift.

29   It's OK that your to-do list will never be all done

Work on Barcelona's famous cathedral, La Sagrada Familia, started 150 years ago and it's still not finished.

My to-do list sometimes feels like Gaudi's cathedral. As much as I cross through the done items, new tasks creep onto the end. It's taken me a while to get comfortable with this concept but – unless you're superhuman – here's the truth: you're never going to get your to-do list done.

There'll be some things you'll never get around to either. That's why I have a column in my to-do app called Someday. I've made peace with Someday. I know I may never get round to it all, but it no longer stresses me out.

Just like that Spanish masterpiece, I fix my mind on what I've got done instead. Perhaps it's pretty impressive just as it is!

30 Be multidimensional at work

In 1986, I went 'plural' for the first time. In an unanticipated gap year before I went to university, I worked part-time for a radio station and a record distribution company. And in between all that, I took a course two afternoons a week in photography.

I loved it! Radio, music and photography was what I was all about. I enjoyed doing – and being – more than one thing. That year informed how I later approached my career: being multidimensional at work.

Why is the world of work obsessed with putting people in boxes? What about if you are more than one thing?

Leonardo Da Vinci was a painter, geologist, cartographer, botanist, musician... the list goes on. His curiosity knew no bounds so he was able to explore everything and anything that interested him.

I've built my career out of mashing-up multiple disciplines, roles and passions. It's led to a range of opportunities I wouldn't otherwise have had.

CHAPTER 2
MAKE IT A HABIT

31   Embrace the spaghetti lines

When you start out, you might plan your career and life journey to follow a neat linear path.

That was my story. If I plotted the first nine years of my career on a graph, it would be a steep line from my humble beginnings as a TV company runner to managing director of a creative business.

But our lives rarely stick to that pattern. We encounter uncertainties or need to deviate from our paths. The trajectory of our lives is spaghetti shaped – curved, knotted, and infinitely malleable.

That's what I learned when I had my burnout. That life comes in a ball of spaghetti – messy at times, but hopefully still tasty – and not in a neat straight line.

32   Have a crazy dream

It was such a hot day and I'd decided to walk to Hyde Park to see The Mastaba, a towering colourful 600-ton pyramid of 55-gallon barrels, floating on the Serpentine Lake.

It was a dream come true for the artists Christo and Jeanne-Claude. They had first had their idea some 40 years earlier. 40 years to realize a dream!

I told this story during a presentation I was giving to students. I told them, have a crazy dream.

Crazy dreams are like beacons. They give us something to head towards and motivate us to try. They fuel entrepreneurs and innovators to make their ideas happen.

In the college auditorium, I asked students to share their dreams. They told me how they wanted to become a fashion stylist, a TV make-up artist, a singer, a games developer. I loved hearing their passion when they spoke about what they wanted to be.

Never let anyone tell you your dreams are unrealistic. Who knows what's possible when you set your heart on something, as wild as it might seem at the time, if you work hard and persevere.

33 Start a self-storytelling habit

Who knew that a scrapbook I made 35 years ago would fuel me today? Occasionally I flick through a scrapbook I collated on my teenage European adventure, a month-long rail trip.

It was 28 days of discovery, self-sufficiency and of following my curiosity.

Me and my friend Tad. A small tent, an even smaller budget. A charity shop tape recorder, a journal, a cheap camera. We enjoyed Florence, Barcelona, Paris. We ate baguettes and drank beer, forged friendships, slept on park benches and outside train stations. We visited the Uffizi, The Venice Biennale.

Everything went into my scrapbook – photos, postcards, tickets, receipts, alongside a journal entry for each day.

Those qualities I learned back then are hallmarks for me today.

When we keep a scrapbook, we are starting a self-storytelling habit. We are laying the bread crumbs, we are laying a trail for who we are, our purpose on the planet. And we can use all this later to find our way in life.

It's not too late to start one today.

34 Stop to listen

If you want to get mindful, you don't have to practise yoga or sit cross-legged on a deserted beach.

You could try something else.

Just stop. And listen.

Do you do that much? Perhaps you stop to listen to the sound of birdsong. Or waves crashing on the beach.

But what about stopping to listen in your busy daily life?

Right now I'm sitting in the Caravan coffee shop in London's Kings Cross. What can I hear?

- Perhaps fifteen, or twenty, conversations layered over each other.
- A bell in the kitchen.
- Pots and pans clatter.
- A teaspoon drops in a saucer.
- A small boy cries out.
- Running water. Or the sizzle of food in a pan?
- Cutlery being sorted into a container. The sound of a cup placed on a saucer.

It's got a rhythm and hum of its very own. My kind of meditation.

35   Sit up at the bar

I'm sitting up at a tapas bar in Bermondsey, south-east London, talking to Miguel. It's his first job in London and he's only been working here six weeks. The smell of the tortilla is making him homesick. It reminds him of his grandmother's cooking back in Spain. She makes a really good tortilla, he says, the best there is.

I only know these details because of where I choose to sit – at what I think is the best seat – up at the bar.

These are only the kind of conversations you can have while a barista is fixing a coffee, or a barman is polishing glasses. You can introduce yourself. You can take time with each other.

If I've a choice, I'll always take a seat at the bar.

36 Dance in the kitchen

Family life can get stressful. Especially when four people – two of them teenagers – are holed up for months home-working and home-schooling.

At lunchtime, during those winter lockdown days of 2020/21, I'd often blast out a cheesy track on the Bluetooth speaker. Irene Cara's 'Flashdance' is a good one. And we'd all throw some wild shapes in the kitchen.

At home, there's no one to impress. It doesn't matter if you look silly, in fact the crazier the better.

It lifted us every time. And brought us closer.

Dancing together is a social glue. Psychologist Dr Peter Lovatt, a.k.a. 'Dr Dance' and author of *The Dance Cure*, has championed the benefits of dance for years. Peter told me that when people dance together (even strangers) four amazing things happen: they report liking each other more, trusting each other and feeling more psychologically similar, and they show more 'pro-social' behaviour.

As Irene Cara sang, 'What a feeling!'

37 Get busy and get on a high!

Sam Ford is a tattoo artist at the top of her game who's worked all over the world. She told me about the thrill of getting back into the tattoo studio as her sector opened up after the pandemic lockdown.

She'd only been back one week but she told me how she loved those intense days in the studio. Sam really thrives when her days are long and busy. She says she's not only most productive but also happiest when she's got lots on. It puts her on a high.

Few things beat that sense of momentum powering through your to-do list when you're on fire and at your best, feeling invincible. Love what you do for a living? Then get busy at work!

38 Unplan your life

I have goals in life. But I don't have a neat, linear plan of how to get there.

At the start of 2020 I had lots of ideas for my business.

But the pandemic erased all my ideas and I had to rethink things.

In a world of uncertainty I think it's futile to have a life plan or a career plan that's set in stone.

No one knows what's around the corner, so why try to guess the future?

Not having a plan means I can go where the water flows. It means I can change course if I see a new opportunity.

My decisions aren't swayed by things not being on my plan. I don't beat myself up that I can't try the path because it wasn't on the plan. I don't have to measure the reality of what I'm doing in business against some arbitrary, made-up plan full of guesses and estimations.

It means I can stay closer to who I am and the work I want to do, that's my compass.

So unplan your life instead.

39 Try a Shultz Hour

George Shultz – who was Secretary of State under President Ronald Reagan – is rumoured to have taken an hour each week to lock himself in the office with only a pad of paper and pen. No interruptions, no tasks at hand to work on, just thinking.

I love that. Thinking time with no distractions feels such a rarity.

What do you imagine you'd achieve with that precious time? Try a Shultz Hour and see what you can achieve.

40 Ask is it a 'Hell Yeah!'?

I have this question from author Derek Sivers pinned above my desk.

'Is it a Hell Yeah?'

It's a fantastic filter for where to put my attention.

Should I go for a swim on the beach? *Hell Yeah!*

Should I take on that project from Sally? *Hell Yeah!*

Should I write this book? *Hell Yeah!*

And if I need to make a decision in my personal or business life and it's not a *Hell Yeah!*, I seriously question whether I say yes to it or not.

41 Make progress

I'm sure you have that same satisfaction as I do when you tick off something from your to-do list. It might be something huge – delivering a year-long project at work or moving house. Or it could be something more mundane – calling the electrician or paying a bill.

But whatever the task, there's that feeling of satisfaction.

And that's what's important to my friend Helen Tupper, co-author of *The Squiggly Career* and co-founder of Amazing If. Helen told me that having a good day is about knowing that her time has been well spent. That sense of achievement.

Helen explained that finishing a project, delivering a talk, or even just completing her list for the day results in the feel-good factor. She gets fulfilment from the progress she's made.

42   Take a Wednesday *Offternoon*

Imagine: your boss says to you on a Wednesday – don't come back to work after lunch. In fact, you don't have to return after lunch on a Wednesday ever again. How cool would that be?

Welcome to the *Offternoon*, an idea pioneered by Kin & Co, a change management company with offices in London and Toronto. Kin & Co's research found that 80 per cent of business owners believed having Wednesday afternoon off could significantly improve productivity. From their own trial of the Wednesday *Offternoon*, they found that a midweek break increased productivity and motivation. They're hoping the idea will catch on with other companies.

What a treat! Wouldn't we be so much more productive, creative and happy having had a midweek afternoon off? What would you do on your Wednesday *Offternoon*?

43   Bring your real self to work

When you arrive at work, does it feel like you need to leave your personality at the door?

Lots of us put on a mask to go to work. But it doesn't have to be this way. Imagine how different life might be if you chose roles – and re-crafted existing ones – that were more You. I believe we'd be happier and more fulfilled.

Michael Burne is founder of Bamboo, a legal services platform. He told me one reason he became an entrepreneur was so he could create a business where he was able to show up as the real him.

Nowhere else he'd worked allowed him to be truly himself at work – so he fixed his own headache and started a business where he could be just that.

If you want to fly, make sure you bring You to work!

44   Walk without a map

The other day a meeting got delayed and I found myself with 30 minutes to spare. Exiting the tube station, I decided to dispense with the map on my iPhone. I knew that Whitecross Street would take me in the right direction northwards and then I'd use my instinct to get me to my destination.

As I walked slowly up the street, I noticed that people on their lunch break were meandering left, and into a little park that I never knew existed. Dotted with office workers, children in a playground and people queuing at a coffee stand, it was a welcome, inspiring break in my day. If I had focused on a map I would have never taken that left turn. It was a detour that happened by just going where the wind blows, or the crowds lead you.

45   Enjoy a micro-exchange

Imagine two scenarios.

One. You enter a café and order a takeaway. It's functional. You scroll through your phone. There's no chat with the barista.

Two. You enter a café and order a takeaway. While waiting, you ask the woman making the coffee about her day. She tells you about the kitten that turned up on her doorstep she's now raising. You walk away with a spring in your step with the thought that things are all right with the world.

These interactions are what Noreena Hertz, author of *The Lonely Century*, describes as 'micro-exchanges'.

Such 30-second exchanges, Hertz writes, help you feel connected with other people and thereby less alone. They can improve our individual and societal wellbeing. These interactions, she says, help you practise how to mix with others and build community. They even contribute to reinforcing our democracies. Asking whether the space is free to put down your yoga mat or chatting with a fellow shopper as you steer your trolley helps you consider other people's views and situations. These moments are more significant than you think.

46   Step away from the last slice

We've all done it – when you've eaten enough but that last slice of pizza is lying on the plate making sad and lonely eyes at you, pleading to be eaten. And you think, I'll do it a favour and put it out of its misery.

But then afterwards you feel leaden and lethargic.

The residents of Okinawa in Japan have a phrase they say to fellow diners before they eat – *hara hachi bu* – which means to eat until 80 per cent full. It's thought that this is one reason the Okinawans have the greatest longevity of any community in the world. How often do you eat until you're full, stuffed, satiated?

Anyway, the pizza will taste even better if you eat it cold the next day...

47 Make it a habit

When you make something a habit it can be powerful. It's self-reinforcing.

When I say to myself I'm going to abstain from alcohol Monday to Thursday and then I repeat that week after week, it becomes a habit I'm less likely to break. It becomes easier to adhere to. If I'm not expecting that taste of a beer after a hard day's work on a Tuesday, I won't miss it.

The same with other habits in our life – if something works we'll stick to it or repeat it. And that's when it becomes powerful – when these little habits become part of your recipe for success or for having a good day.

48 Tune in to those two-inch events

When the co-founder of the animation company Pixar, Ed Catmull, was a child, his family was in a car accident on a winding canyon road. Two inches to the left and the car would have gone over the cliff. Two inches – no Ed. No Pixar!

Just think. No *Toy Story*, no *Inside Out*, no *Up!*

In his book *Creativity Inc*, Ed describes this as a two-inch moment.

Let's tune into those events where you are two inches from misadventure and two inches from opportunity. So many of the trajectories in my life have been that close. Two inches from an Aaagh. But also two inches from a Wooaah!

On a Sunday evening in August 2003, the very last day of my ten-day internet dating trial subscription, I decided to check the dating website one final time. I guess it was one of those moments when I nearly didn't bother (definitely two inches either way).

The site suggested I was a good match with 'Zoë from Streatham'.

I clicked on her.

She's my wife ;)

49   Give a shit, but give zero f***s!

I was reading a profile of The Who in *Rolling Stone* magazine.

The journalist Stephen Rodrick was travelling with Pete Townshend and Roger Daltrey in 2019, and one thought kept coming back to him.

He noticed that they give zero f***s. But he explained this should not be mistaken for not giving a shit. They still care about their music and putting in the effort.

I love that.

That's what I strive for.

I like the correlation between 'giving a shit' but at the same time 'giving zero f***s'.

To care. To have a work ethic. But not trying to please everyone and doing things your way.

50   Find your superpower

As a young boy of around nine years old I remember feeling like the outsider: the kid standing at the playground edges rather than at the heart of the action.

But I learned that the edge wasn't a bad place to stand. I liked to observe the world around me, spending my time doing impressions of teachers, doodling and sketching classroom scenes rather than pay attention in class.

And that sense of being the outsider is my superpower!

Those early experiences have been invaluable – they have helped me be resilient, objective, dispassionate. Being the outsider is why people hire me, why people come to my talks and workshops. An outsider viewpoint brings a fresh perspective; a good vantage point for storytelling; a position to observe, take it all in and see clearly.

It runs through me like a message through a stick of rock. What's your superpower?

51 Try a self-induced laugh

There's a lovely audio clip of BBC newsreader Charlotte Green getting the giggles in a live news bulletin. She normally demonstrates great gravitas, so to hear her unable to control herself is quite a moment. I've probably played that 20 or 30 times and it still makes me laugh.

Trying to laugh more often – even if it is self-induced – is a recommendation from psychologist Paul McGhee in his book *Humor as Survival Training for a Stressed-Out World*. He says creating opportunities where you can laugh more often is really good for your health, even if you just do it by yourself. Paul also suggests you surround yourself with humour.

Do you have some clips that consistently make you laugh even though you have seen or heard them before?

52 Make time for it

Whenever I travel out of Paddington railway station I like to get a coffee before I board the train. But the booths on the station concourse only offer a transactional experience: the coffee tastes substandard and there's nowhere nice to sit.

That's why I have my 'Paddington rule.'

Two minutes' walk from the station is Kioskafé, run by *Monocle* magazine. Here I can get a quality cup of coffee, sit if I fancy it, and can browse the hundreds of magazines they have on sale. And they have a really cool Japanese loo.

Having done this a dozen or so times I can tell you it makes a big difference to the rest of my day. Now I make sure I get there early enough to pop in. It's worth it every time.

53   End the day with a *Feierabend*

Are we working from home? Or living at work? It's a conundrum many of us wrestle with – when to down tools and turn our surroundings back into homes again. With this in mind, it's good to 'bookend' the working day and create boundaries.

The Germans have a word for marking the moment when you switch off at work for the day: the *Feierabend*. It's a celebration that your work is done and is often accompanied by a German beer.

Often during the week I'll head out for a short walk with the dog, to clear my head and get back into dad and husband mode. On Fridays I'll go for a German version when I'll snap the top off a beer, crank up the music and celebrate the end of the week. It's often harder to delineate work from home, requiring you to be more intentional to shift your mindset.

What would work for you? Ten minutes' meditation? Lighting a candle? Even reading a fiction book for a few minutes?

54 Choose who you let into your headphones

As I write this I'm listening to the magical sounds of Ballaké Sissoko playing the kora. It's beautiful. Peaceful.

And a reminder about who you let into your ears.

You wouldn't invite just anyone in through your front door would you?

So why are you letting that newscaster, arrogant podcast guest or toxic politician into your home or headphones?

Sometimes we forget that we have a choice about what we consume.

I care about what I let in – it affects my quality of day.

That's why, long ago, I swapped a particular radio news show in the morning for a combination of Radio 3 and BBC 6 Music.

I did not want to have politicians arrogantly giving blithe answers and polluting the airspace in my kitchen.

Careful who you open the front door of your mind to.

55 Act 'as if'

A long time ago I read a book called *The Naked Leader* by David Taylor.

There's one piece of advice from it that's stayed with me all these years.

The author says that the fastest way to make any change in your life is to act *as if* the change has already been made. Your mind cannot tell the difference between something that happens in reality and something you imagine with emotional intensity.

Let's pretend you lack confidence when it comes to public speaking.

So applying David's advice, think about how different it might be if you acted *as if* you were a master at it. Pretend you've got it nailed, and you might convince yourself you can do it.

Acting *as if* – it can be a sneaky tool in your armoury.

56 Find your spiritual home

There's something about Amsterdam. It's a place that fuels me, where I feel most me. I must have visited twenty times. On the one hand, the street names look so familiar. But with their Grachts and Straats, it also feels a world away.

I love the architecture and the canals. So many windows I pass seem to invite me in – they are open and bare from curtains or blinds. It's a certain kind of confidence that's on display. Residents happily get on with their lives, visible to passers-by: a woman brings a pot from the kitchen over to the table; a woman eats soup as she reads a newspaper. A curled-up cat lazily eyes the street scene; a dog snoozes on cushions on a bench.

Through these unshuttered windows I glimpse those signs of daily activity that are, to me, signs of a healthy and good life: bicycles, coffee machines, wine bottles, books, pictures on the wall and vases of flowers. This openness is so attractive. It mirrors my own desire for open, honest and authentic relationships in my life.

I guess I love Amsterdam because to me it feels like home.

57 Dial up the brightness switch

Since he started meditating, Michael Acton Smith has seen huge benefits in his working life. It's given him the ability to make better decisions in work. To have more perspective and more clarity.

As co-founder of Calm – an app that has now been downloaded more than 100 million times – Michael is looking to change perceptions around the idea of meditation. That you don't need to sit in the lotus position wearing an orange robe – it's something you can do on an app on the tube or in the back of a taxi.

I asked Michael what difference meditation has made to his life. Now, he says, he's increased his awareness and thoughtfulness about everything going on around him. He's become more conscious of how he uses his phone. He's become more tuned in to the thoughts that race through his mind, and can now stop them sucking him down rabbit holes. He says he's in more control of his mind – as opposed to previously it controlled him.

Michael says that developing a meditation practice and living more mindfully is like dialling up the brightness switch on life.

58 Don't eat the whole chocolate bar

I read an interview with the explorer Erling Kagge where he talked about the essentials he takes on an expedition. And how at the top of a mountain or on an arduous journey, a single piece of chocolate tastes better than an entire bar.

I like that philosophy.

A deep hit of espresso over a big pot of coffee?

One glass of wine to savour instead of the whole bottle to glug?

One night in a five star luxury resort that's appreciated rather than two weeks that could be taken for granted?

Sometimes a sliver is just enough.

59 Write it down!

I am obsessive about to-do lists.

From scheduling important calls to buying a lightbulb. It all goes on a list.

It's David Allen – the author of *Getting Things Done* – who says your brain is for having ideas, not storing information. I've lived by that mantra for many years and have found it wildly useful, if not essential.

After I've had the shower or arrived back from a dog walk, I'll grab a scrap of paper and note down whatever thought or idea has just come to mind. And then I'll transfer it into my to-do list app, TeuxDeux, which sits across all my devices.

TeuxDeux was created by Brooklyn-based entrepreneur Tina Roth Eisenberg. Tina told me she built it primarily for herself in order to get all those 3am thoughts out of her head.

Making lists. It's my single biggest hack for getting things done.

60 Start your day on a front foot

You know that feeling when you have a lot to get done?

And then perhaps you wake up earlier than usual – or you set the alarm early – the sun is shining and you feel motivated to get up while everyone else is asleep.

So you go for that run, you clean out the fridge, or you get that difficult email written.

And then it's done.

That's a great feeling. Ticking one or two things off your to-do list first-thing can create a positive mindset for the rest of the day.

That sense of 'come on – bring it on!'

Those early wins will stay with you for the rest of the day.

CHAPTER 3
COUNT THE THINGS THAT COUNT

61   Keep your lightbulb shining bright

There's a bar I used to go to near Oxford Circus called The Social. The bare lightbulbs that hung over each table were controlled by your own dimmer switch, so you could turn the intensity up or down.

When you do work that fuels you, in line with your passions, the brilliance of your lightbulb increases. And when you put your attention on things that aren't you – projects or people that aren't right for you – the light diminishes.

Your lightbulb is the signal for the things in life that lift you and bring you joy.

Recognizing that signal helps you make the right choices about what you do and how you spend your time.

When does your lightbulb burn brightly, and when is it dimmed? What are the things or people that light you up? And what are those that take you away from You? Because when it dims, your presence in the world is dulled too. And people aren't able to see the true, illuminated You.

62   What gets your lightbulb shining bright?

Exercise

On a piece of paper make two columns headed 'Dim' and 'Shine'.

Make a list here of the things that deplete you, that dim your bulb, and those that energize you, that make your bulb shine bright.

Know what you need to do to get your bulb shining bright.

63   Sneak into an art gallery

If you live or work close to an art gallery or museum – especially one that's free to enter – it's so easy to pop in for a quick visit.

You don't always need to allocate lots of time – a lunch break can be long enough to reap the benefits.

Some days when there's time between meetings I wander into Tate Modern. One Monday afternoon I chanced upon Marwan Rechmaoui's giant map of Beirut. Embossed into rubber on the floor, it's for walking over – a symbol of the city's resilience. It was beautifully quiet in the space and I had the exhibit to myself.

Or I might take the escalator up to the top floor and sit on the big black squashy sofas. I find that vast space inspiring. I can sit and do nothing. And have the space to think.

These little snatches of time at a gallery – it might be 10 minutes or 60 minutes – take you out of the everyday and into something else. It can plunge you into a feast of someone else's ideas and concepts, or simply give you the space to dream. It always makes a difference to my day.

64   Rate things out of ten

I write down the good things (see Idea #3) which gives me a fantastic metric for guiding my choices. David Kelley's way is another version of looking at things.

In the book *Creative Confidence* by David and his brother Tom, David tells the story of the experiment he tried when he got cancer. He started rating what he'd done each day. He noted that driving along in the car singing out loud to music scored high; going to faculty meetings scored low. So David started singing more and stopped going to so many meetings.

Rate out of ten each thing you do every day. And then note what drives you up to a ten.

65 Get some plasters

The notion of having more good days is not about ignoring the hard parts of your life. Some days are going to be better than others. It's about taking positive action to notice, celebrate and amplify the good bits.

It's also about knowing there'll be falls and scrapes along the way. So dig out the plasters.

You are not going to emerge from this great venture of life unscathed.

That's okay.

You can't avoid the bumps and scrapes. But you can be there to pick yourself up again afterwards. Stick on a band-aid. It's time to get going again.

66 Count the things that count

I'm leafing through my 'Good Times' lists from one particular month a few years back. Turning the pages and finding so much joy in the everyday family life.

Walking my sons to school. Giving a talk at a university. Sitting by the fire. Reading the kids a story. Making a roasted feta salad. A pub lunch. Doodling in a notepad on the train.

Wow. It looked like a really special month. So many wonderful memories.

After smiling at all those memories, next I went through my old spreadsheets to find my income for that same month. What had I invoiced? And I can tell you, it was pretty dismal.

So the question is: was I successful that month?

How you decide to view your life is up to you. I know how I view mine.

67 Marie-Kondo your life

Marie Kondo has made a career from instructing people to tidy up, only keeping the possessions and clothes that make you happy – or, in her words, 'spark joy' – and to ditch the rest.

It's an interesting concept, not one I can always adhere to, because I love a home full of books.

What else can this philosophy apply to? We trot along in life often not considering elements that are no longer useful. There might be some old friendships you've outgrown, or some kinds of work you're doing that drag you down. We don't often consciously pay attention to these things, but sometimes it's good to take stock and cull those elements that no longer contribute to our joy.

Maybe it's time to Marie-Kondo those too?

68 Live in a city where life happens outside

Sejal and her partner didn't fancy bringing their young family back to London after having lived in California for three years.

They drew up a shortlist of European cities they'd like to move to and decided on Barcelona. The diversity of people and culture was one key element, plus the proximity of the sea and nature, as well as being easy to travel out of, for work and visiting family. The weather also appealed, and what that meant for interacting with the city.

It's liberating, Sejal says, to see friends outdoors. They don't need plans to go to someone's apartment or book an indoors activity. The city squares, superblocks and pedestrianization enable natural or incidental interactions.

Sejal likes it that, when city life happens outside, she can see all slices and generations of society co-existing. In Barcelona she sees life happening right in front of her. She feels part of something.

69 Take a break!

In Dan Pink's book *When: The Scientific Secrets of Perfect Timing*, the author cites data from two parole boards in Israel, where judges were sitting all day to hear prisoners' cases. The research found that the judges started each session being lenient, ruling in favour of the prisoners. But as time went on, they ruled against the prisoners, regardless of the facts of the case.

The interesting thing is that when the judges then take a break, on returning to the courtroom they become more lenient again. A pattern emerged where at the start of a session, or after a break, the judges are more forgiving.

I'm guessing that few of your work choices involve a prisoner's freedom. Yet whatever project you have in front of you, taking a break from it will help you have a clearer head and more focus. Even if that feels counterintuitive as you're stuck in the middle of a task – step away.

70 Get creative with the definition of 'creative'

My best creative experience recently? An impromptu Sunday afternoon project with my son. He wanted to replace the broken backboard on his basketball net. It might sound simple enough, but with rusted, weather-beaten bolts and screws, it took a lot of perseverance, a drill, a piece of wood, a saw and a trip to the DIY shop.

I loved the challenge, I loved working with my son and I loved the feeling that happens when you get lost in a task, not thinking about anything else.

We stood back, shot some hoops, proud of what we'd created.

71   Give someone a real-life 'Like'

One morning I surprised myself by doing something I certainly hadn't thought about doing, and I'd never done before.

I chased an MP down the street.

I was in a Pret a Manger near Westminster enjoying a coffee with Nick when I glimpsed someone familiar walking by. I apologized to Nick, dashed out of the door and ran down the road. It was a well-known MP who had recently taken – in my view – an admirable stand on an issue. I called out his name, caught up with him and said 'thank you'. I shook his hand.

I know MPs and those in public service get given a hard time. I'd never chased an MP down the street to thank them before, but sometimes it's worth giving people in public service a real-life 'Like'.

72   Get fuzzy by giving something away

I'd bought us a family travelcard for the tube: it was valid for two adults and two children, unlimited travel around Greater London for the whole day.

We'd reached our destination by mid-morning so didn't need the travelcard anymore.

In the long queues for ticket machines at Kings Cross station I approached a family waiting in line. Do you want a travelcard? I asked them. You can have it for free.

And as I passed it over the barrier, I got that warm and fuzzy feeling inside that almost makes your hair stand on end. It took me by surprise, that I felt it so strongly. I often get that hair-raise when on stage and I reveal the punchline of a story.

But with a travelcard?! I was somewhat surprised. But it just goes to show, it feels good to give things away.

73   Go sit on a bench

In his book *In Praise Of Wasting Time*, Alan Lightman tells the story of when he was a physics student at Caltech (the California Institute of Technology). There was a guy called Paul who used to spend hours sitting on a bench.

While other students were working on equations or soldering in the lab, Paul sat for hours. He did it so much, he'd get a look of disapproval from the passing professors.

Who's the Paul on the bench?

His name is Paul L. Schechter and he went on to become a famous astronomer and observational cosmologist, being awarded the Guggenheim Fellowship for Natural Sciences. And he got his ideas and even made a number of important cosmological discoveries by – yes, you guessed it – sitting on that bench.

74   Be an idea collector

If you want to be better at coming up with ideas, start by collecting old ones.

Take a notebook everywhere, or use your phone to capture thoughts and ideas. Write down your own thoughts on your morning train commute.

Note other people's ideas and stories, copy quotes that inspire you, cut things out, snap photos on your phone.

On his travels around the world, fashion designer Paul Smith takes photographs of everything from street scenes to window displays. Such images inform his next collection.

The act of clipping (whether with a digital tool or a pair of scissors) makes my brain well-tuned to spotting inspiring content, whether it's a blog post, a tweet, a newspaper article or a photo in a magazine. It's satisfying to have a portfolio of ideas to leaf through when you're looking for inspiration. I never know when these may come in handy.

75   Go behind the scenes

You know that feeling when you come to the end of a cherished novel or favourite TV show and you feel bereft it's all over?

One thing I've started doing when the end titles roll or I close the book is to keep my hunger fed a bit longer by going 'behind the scenes'.

I check out the author or creator. Having finished Adam Haslett's book *Imagine Me Gone*, I found a video clip from the Chicago Humanities Festival in which he discusses the book.

On finishing Taffy Brodesser-Akner's excellent book *Fleishman Is in Trouble*, I dived into the video recording of a 60-minute Q&A the author did at a bookstore in Washington DC. When I explore more deeply an author's or filmmaker's intent, it adds to my understanding as well as giving me a deeper layer of interest to the experience.

So if you love something – a show, a book, a piece of music – once you're done with it, unpack the story behind the story.

76   Pick up the phone

This morning I needed to update Rachel, a collaborator on a project. It felt fairly complex to distil into an email.

Instead, I picked up the phone. And we had a conversation.

Clear and simple.

There was no cc, no bcc, no bullet points, just a human-to-human conversation.

The idea of picking up the phone and calling someone seems to have become so revolutionary! But when every online meeting is a video call, or when so much of communication is WhatsApp, Slack or text messages, it's liberating to cut through all the tech and simply call someone.

77   Launch it now

Having the idea is (relatively) easy. Doing something about it is the hard part.

That's what I like about Michael Mentessi. He just dives in and does it.

Michael lives in my town. Ten years ago we were having coffee together when he asked me if I knew of any local meetup groups for creatives, freelancers and small businesses. I didn't.

We should start one of our own, he suggested.

I nodded in agreement.

I guess most people might have left that idea there, to follow up at some stage in the future, but not Michael. He pulled out his laptop, punched in Meetup.com and – right there and then – registered a group. We wrote the description. We chose a time. We selected a venue. We hit the launch button.

And the Meetup group is still going strong, all these years later.

All down to Michael's spirit of not just having an idea, but doing something about it.

78   Savour the little days

I can recall one of the Sanders family's favourite days. A sunny Saturday when we ate breakfast, lunch and dinner outside. My wife and I pottered around in the garden. The kids played together. The afternoon came, the wine was uncorked and we sat reading the weekend papers.

That experience was one of the best days of my life (no doubt about it). It wasn't planned, it just happened. There was no red carpet film premiere, there was no party on a billionaire's private yacht, no holiday of a lifetime, just the four of us in our garden.

Oh I have crap days too (no doubt about it). Things don't go to plan, we get served curveballs, voices get raised. But days that don't go smoothly throw ones like this particular Saturday into sharp relief, and it was made all the sweeter. It was just a little day, nothing grand, where the stars aligned, one to savour.

79   Find calm in the stress

Millions of people use his app every day.

But Calm.com only came into being because its co-founder – Michael Acton Smith – was having a difficult time with stress.

Over a pot of tea on the roof of Shoreditch House, Michael told me his philosophy: that life is short and wonderful, so we need to make the most of it. He wants to squeeze as much juice out of it as he can.

But he found if you squeeze too much juice, it can be problematic.

Back in the early 2010s he was getting off on the adrenaline rush of being an entrepreneur, putting in 14 to 16 hour days, working weekends.

A turning point came in 2014 when he decided to go on holiday by himself for the first time. His mind for once was away from the office and work. He instead read up on mindfulness and meditation. A lightbulb went on. During this week of downtime he discovered how meditation is a kind of superpower, a smart way of looking after our minds.

Had he not given himself time off, Calm.com might not have launched. Good ideas happen when you step back to take a breath, not wringing every minute out of every day.

80   Be like a fine wine

In a *Harvard Business Review* post, Chip Conley writes that as you get older you can sometimes feel like an old carton of milk, approaching its expiration date. But rather than sour milk, he likens getting old – and the experience you bring in life and work – to bottles of fine wine and the appreciation that comes with it.

It's a good way of looking at ageing. As I write, I'm 52 years old, the same age Chip Conley was when he joined Airbnb as an advisor. Chip's the author of *Wisdom At Work: The Making of a Modern Elder*. He writes about that experience joining Airbnb, where most people were decades younger than him. But what Chip found was that he was able to bring his full life experience to the company. And now he's building a whole movement around the notion of being an elder.

Remember maturity means having lived, and all the wisdom, skills and benefit that comes with it. Breathe into the role of being a bottle of fine wine, and embrace how you finesse as you get older.

81 Luxury isn't always expensive

We were staying in a lovely hotel overlooking a pretty bay.

I sat on the terrace and looked out. I noticed that the two cliffs on either side of the harbour looked like they were hugging the bay, as if they were two arms protecting us, cosseting us from the outside world.

Staying at this hotel we knew this little private world – of service with a smile and ice cold glasses of *rosado* sitting by the pool – could not be forever. So we drank it in.

But you know what? Down the road was a small tatty roof terrace bar. It was unremarkable from the outside, and cramped for space. But we found a spot sitting on cushions on its concrete steps. We ordered a couple of cheap drinks and got our boys some snacks. We sat and chatted, listening to the 90s music being played. We could still look out over the harbour and from our unglamourous spot we watched the sun go down. That was the best night of the holiday – that was real luxury.

82 Be your Badass!

One of Harvard Business School's more unusual offerings is a short course for MBA students called 'Anatomy of a Badass'.

Led by professors Francesco Gino and Frances X. Frei, it's about being unapologetically bold and authentic at work. The course used the example of the marketing leader Bozoma Saint John, who's worked at Netflix, Uber and Apple.

Bozoma says she has found success by celebrating what makes her different and then, unashamedly, she brings those things to work.

The professors claim that being your true 'Badass' self can lead to greater performance professionally as well as increased personal satisfaction, helping interviewees win the job and entrepreneurs get funding for their venture.

So, get Badass!

83 Stretch yourself to grow

Last year, I really stretched myself. Stretched in a good way: pushing myself to new heights, venturing into new territory, constantly moving forwards and embracing new opportunities.

When you stretch yourself, the end result will go one of two ways: you'll either pull it off or it will fall flat.

The irony is, of course, that you'll never know you can do it until you do it.

But what's the other option? If you choose not to stretch yourself, to stay safe and comfortable, that's fine. But when you do that there's no opportunity for growth, for seeing where you might go, for having adventures in different scenarios.

It's one of life's pleasures, surmounting a hurdle to achieve success; doing something difficult and pulling it off.

84 Look for awe and you'll smile more

In a study by the University of California, a group of 60–90-year-olds was asked to take a weekly 15-minute walk outdoors for eight weeks. Half the group was told to look out for awe, while the other half was given no instructions. Both were told to take a photo of themselves on their walk.

The research showed that the people who went on the awe-walk displayed more positive emotions than the others. They even displayed a greater smile intensity in their selfies across the eight-week period.

85 Seek out the Steves

Life's too short to work with people who don't get you.

So it's worth taking the time to seek out the good people.

Meet Steve Clayton. Steve is a fellow Brit working for one of the world's biggest and most famous companies, based in the Pacific Northwest.

When I discovered him online, I liked his spirit. Even though he's in a senior role at a big corporation, his personality and passions are still evident. He's passionate about design and magazines. He loves the band New Order (always a good sign). A snowboarder.

Hmm, Steve is the kind of bloke I'd like to go for a beer with, I thought.

But also to work with.

That was a few years ago.

It wasn't until last year that I finally reached out to him. I sent him a handwritten note on a postcard I picked up at the Design Museum. It led to me interviewing him for a video series side project. Then he recommended me for a project and subsequently asked me to do a talk for his colleagues.

Look for the Steves.

86 Carry a camera

I love walking around cities taking photographs, whether with my vintage 35mm camera or my phone. It sharpens my curiosity – I'm always observing and noticing details, spotting things I hadn't seen before. People gesticulating; quirky signs; ornate shop fronts.

Inhibition goes out the viewfinder when I look at the world through a lens. Put a camera around my neck and I will get in all sorts of uncomfortable positions – crouching on the pavement to get that perfect shot of that vintage Fiat 500. I'm in my element when the familiar weight of my 1982 Pentax K1000 sits against my body, when I hear that reassuring click of the shutter.

Being able to look at the world through a camera is sacred to me. Slowing down to notice, expressing my creativity and looking at things differently is a way of framing my world, both literally and metaphorically. Taking photos is an extension of who I am, another limb or organ even; a way to live and breathe, and be present.

87 Find a secret playground

When the kids were small we took them to Copenhagen. What we loved about this city was the number of playgrounds. There seemed to be one around every corner. So handy for a toddler and four-year-old.

One afternoon we were walking around the neighbourhood of Vesterbro. It had been raining all day and the boys were getting bored.

We came across a huge wall with an unassuming gate. No idea what was behind it we pushed the gate and, wow, we emerged into Skydebanehaven. It was something out of a fairytale, like we'd discovered a secret playground. Situated in an old shooting range, it featured a huge slide, climbing ropes and a zip wire. The children were in their element. And on a holiday like that, if the kids are happy, then it follows that the adults are too. A gift.

88 Enjoy being part of a team

In January 2015, I was hired for a one-off, week-long project in a team and with an organization I'd never worked with before. I was away from home, in another country. The days were long and the work intense.

The surroundings weren't what I was used to. I was thrown in at the deep end.

I have to admit – the first few days were completely draining. I was well and truly out of my comfort zone, feeling alone and unsure of myself.

But once I'd settled in, I started to enjoy it.

What turned it around for me? It was that human element, being part of a team. Working hard, but exchanging a laugh across the room. Going out for dinner with everyone. Laughing afterwards in a bar.

Thank you Olly, Jenny, Ross, Mike, Jose, Adrian, Paul, Gay, Micol and Henry for making me welcome and reminding me why teams work.

89 Think like a kid

Once, in the 1990s, my French friend Alain came to visit. Alain had never eaten Japanese food before, so I took him out to my local restaurant. Halfway through the meal he went to find the toilet. When he hadn't returned after fifteen minutes, I got up to look for him.

I discovered him in the kitchen! He was quizzing the chefs about the food and its preparation.

That made me smile.

I'd been to the restaurant a few times before but had never met the chef. Yet on Alain's first visit he simply walked in there and started asking questions. His curiosity was almost childlike and totally uninhibited. Few of us would think it appropriate to walk into a restaurant kitchen uninvited. But perhaps next time your interest is piqued about how something is made, let your curiosity get the better of you, and ask.

90 Befriend your emotions

When you're feeling sad, anxious or having a bad day, what steps can you take?

The starting point, according to clinical psychologist Dr Hazel Harrison, is to get friendly with your emotions. Emotions are sources of information – they help you navigate your day. Being more accurate with what you're feeling allows you to be clearer about what you can do.

Next comes acceptance. Knowing that it's okay not to be okay. Then, recognize that you're not the only person feeling that way – when you realize others are likely to be experiencing the same things, it gives you a connection.

Then, Hazel says, think how you would speak to someone you really care about who was going through a tough time. You probably have compassionate words for others – it's time for self-compassionate words to yourself. So think, what would you say to them? What would help them feel better? Then, say those things to yourself.

CHAPTER 4
VIEW LIFE AS A ROAD TRIP

91   *Kintsugi* your life

In the Japanese art of *kintsugi*, broken pieces of pottery are repaired using lacquer enhanced with gold, silver or platinum. The streaks of precious metal that run through the bowls and vases adds to their beauty. Perhaps some would say the items are no longer perfect – but those repaired cracks give an additional layer of attractiveness.

It's a wonderful metaphor for thinking about your life. How your own cracks and imperfections make you who you are. That there is beauty in your quirks, anxiety or vulnerability.

So rather than hide your flaws away, let's be honest about them. We're all broken to a degree. We've had to pick ourselves up or patch ourselves back together. For some it's a little, for others it's a lot.

It is your imperfections that make you unique, and how you've mended yourself that makes you shine.

92   Don't defer your happiness

The dominant career model of the twentieth century was that we'd work for four decades and then retire. All those grand plans to take a big trip or follow your dream would be deferred until later in your life.

But in the 2020s, the traditional concept of retirement has passed its use-by date. Most of us will be working into our old age.

We're mostly all going to be working harder for a lot longer. Who knows where you'll be in a decade. Let's embrace that spirit of living in the now, and not putting off your hopes and dreams until later.

93 View life as a road trip

If we're truly honest, we're all really just trying to find our way in life. We're all on a journey: sometimes we know where we're headed, other times not.

The road trip is my perfect analogy: you start off in life without a clear map but knowing you're heading somewhere, needing to stop to refuel, getting lost, maybe picking up a few fellow travellers on the way, negotiating busy main roads and bumpy tracks.

Seeing life as a road trip, you can embrace the magic that happens off the beaten track, on the side roads, by taking left turns and following your curiosity. The people you'll meet, the random adventures you'll have. If you focus on your travels rather than on obsessing about an end point, you can enjoy the journey better. The destination may well be elusive, one you'll never reach.

Are you enjoying your road trip? Is it time for a random turn?

94 Skip the conference session

When you invest time and money going to a conference, the obvious way to spend your day is glued to what's happening inside the convention centre. You've come all this way, so you don't want to miss anything.

But what if the value lies outside the convention centre, in those ramblings and conversations beyond the planned schedule?

On the last day of a conference in Amsterdam, I skipped the programme to spend two hours with Karen Wickre, a work friend who's based in San Francisco. She didn't know the city well so I welcomed the chance to show her my highlights. We started at the Athenaeum Niewscentrum magazine store, then toured the three floors of the American Book Center, before walking to Foam, my favourite photography gallery.

We enjoyed a leisurely coffee in the basement café, not looking at our watches, not worried about where we were meant to be. And then we visited the exhibits upstairs.

I don't know what I may have missed back at the conference. But I do know that I had a great couple of hours with someone who I don't usually get the chance to spend time with.

95 Find someone you can be all of You with

It was a rare night away from the children, the chance for my wife and I to wander around a city and take time to be.

'Do you know why you're my best friend?' I asked Zoë as we sat up in the window in Strangers coffee shop in Norwich.

'Because with you, I can be all of me.'

I see it like a pie chart. Some people in your life only get to see a selection of the slices in your pie chart. With my wife Zoë, she gets all of my slices.

She lets me be me.

Why does it matter? When you can reveal all 360 degrees of yourself – those interests, talents, passions, values and traits – you are you in all your complicated glory, the good bits as well as the flaws.

To have someone that accepts all of that is freeing.

96 Do what is right and true

I guess most of us will have moments in life when we feel lost, where we don't know where to go next.

It can be an unsettling feeling.

But perhaps you can take comfort from knowing that feeling lost is part of being human.

My friend Jerry Colonna has a lovely take on it.

He asks, what if being lost is part of the path? What if feeling lost, directionless and uncertain of the progress is an indicator of growth?

In his book *Reboot! Leadership and the Art of Growing Up*, Jerry suggests giving up the need for measurable progress. Instead, he says, focus on doing what is right and true each day. This way, you'd live in congruence with your truest self, where the meaning of your life is a function of the meaning of each day. And each day, an expression of your life.

I think that's beautiful.

Doing what is 'right and true' each day. What does that look like for you?

97 Look for the answers in the streets

When you're looking for answers in your life, you might pick up a book, search online or ask a friend. You probably don't tend to look around the streets. Street Wisdom, a walking-workshop concept started by David Pearl and Chris Barez-Brown, aims to change that. Street Wisdom turns urban streets into a creative playground, using the built-up surroundings to unlock fresh thinking and find answers to whatever you're struggling with. The premise is simple – you ask the street a question and then, by slowing down and noticing, you see what answers come to you. I was invited along to join one of their introductory sessions in 2014 and found it enlightening!

These sessions are run by volunteers and are free to join – check out the Street Wisdom website to see if there's one happening near you.

98 Schedule some self-care

Every Sunday evening my friend Kelly Hoey has a self-care routine – and it's sacred.

On a call from her New York apartment, she said sometimes it might be reading a book or watching a movie. Quite often it involves harnessing the benefits of an infrared blanket. It works like a portable, at-home sauna to get rid of toxins, soothe pain and boost the immune system. Kelly swears by, as she describes it, getting wrapped up like a burrito and sweating out the week!

Kelly invests a lot of energy into her projects and speaking engagements so she knows she needs to look after herself. Whether it's downtime that involves a novel or her blanket ritual, it marks the end of the weekend and gets her set up for the week ahead.

99 Gather people together

A favourite moment from my professional life was when I ran a workshop in London with the Do Lectures. The workshop was on how to make a success of working for yourself. We had 25 people in the room, mostly from the UK, but a couple had come from as far as Oslo and New York.

I'd spent a long time designing a great line-up for the day-long session. But the real value? The people in the room, the feedback that they shared and the connections that were made.

When the workshop ended Nick suggested going to the pub (well it was a Friday!).

As I joined them inside Camden's Edinboro Castle pub, it was great to see everyone – who'd only just met that morning – having a good chat.

Today they're still in touch, supporting each other or making plans to meet again.

100 Follow the crumbs

Judi Oates has a senior role in the leadership team of a bank. She's at a stage in her career where there is no external pressure on her to learn anything new. Yet Judi always embraces a learning mindset, whether that's reading about something outside her sphere of knowledge, taking a journey of discovery, or heading to Spain to attend a leadership course.

I wondered what's driving her in this learning mindset. The organization isn't asking her to do this. It's not something her boss told her to do. On a video call from her home in South Wales, Judi explained that it's part of her personality. She's a seeker. She told me she has an insatiable drive that means she's always searching for something and excited about learning something new.

She is naturally curious, 'following the crumbs' to uncover what sparks her curiosity, meandering down random paths to discover something new. When some parts of her job are tedious, she likes the treat of following the crumbs to balance the more mundane parts.

101 Set rewards to look forward to

A visit to the gym, a glass of wine, a trip to your favourite clothes shop.

When you have your head down and the pressure is on, it can be really motivating to think about what you can look forward to when you're done.

Perhaps you're half-way through an online course, going through a really busy spell at work, or you're dealing with a challenging matter in your personal life.

Looking forward to the treat when you cross the finish line – getting the qualification, emerging from under a pile of envelopes, submitting the pitch on time – can spur you on to get through the tough times. A reward well-deserved is all the sweeter for it too.

102 Take a *fika* break

I know of a team that goes out of the office together once a week. At 3pm on a Thursday they take a half hour break for coffee and pastries. You mustn't schedule a meeting then – because they're making time for *fika*.

Fika is a Swedish workplace tradition where colleagues take a break together for coffee and cake. And work chat is strictly off limits.

My friend Sally hosts regular online *fika* sessions with her team around the world. She told me it's a wonderful way to get to know one another – with no agenda other than having those real, human conversations and asking each other how they are. She says it's often the highlight of her week.

103 Create time affluence

Laurie Santos is professor of psychology at Yale University. A few years ago I took her online course 'The Science of Well-Being', where Professor Santos shared an example of an experiment she'd conducted. Once, before a college lecture she was giving, the professor handed out flyers saying that the class was cancelled and that students had one hour to do whatever they wanted. They were not allowed to do any studies but were to use the time freely to go for a walk, meet a friend or read a book.

One student was so grateful for this gift of time, she started to cry.

Many people I know rush around and say they're so busy that they don't have enough time for what they want to do. Professor Santos' example here demonstrates how time affluence – a sense of being wealthy of time – can boost your happiness.

What would you give up to grab an extra hour? Getting up earlier? Cancelling a non-urgent appointment? Forgoing a TV programme? If the thought of reclaiming time makes you feel like that student and want to cry – then you know it's important!

104 Meet one new person a week

In the 1990s when I started my working life, lots of colleagues had a Rolodex on their desk, a rotating device used to store contact information. When you'd meet a new person, you'd fill out a new card and slot it in the correct spot.

If you hang out with the same people, inside and outside of work, you can get stale. You know your contacts' opinions and their outlook. You can second guess what's going to come out of their mouths next.

Some years ago I started an experiment. I set myself a goal of meeting one new person a week. One memorable encounter was a meeting with dancer and choreographer Zoi Dimitriou, who was taking part in an artists' residency locally. On the surface Zoi and I had little in common. But once we got talking, there were so many shared experiences and emotions. It was a conversation that really opened my eyes.

Making new contacts, going out of my comfort zone, learning lessons from other worlds, and the serendipity that can come from random connections – it's a great way to stay fresh and interested in the wider world. Get your virtual Rolodex out and start adding cards!

105 Fall in love with an orange stapler

Last month a small parcel arrived at our house. It was a stapler my wife had discovered, in my favourite colour – orange. It's called the 'Klizia' and is made by an Italian company, Ellepi. The creation of stationery designer Oscar Lepre, it's shaped like a whale to reflect his love of the ocean. That's it. A piece of metal. It emits small staples that hold pieces of paper together.

It's not going to win any global innovation awards, but it wins an award from me for brightening my desk and brightening my day. Just because something's functional doesn't mean it can't bring a bit of joy into your life.

106 Always travel with a notepad

I get energized whenever I'm on a journey somewhere new, or in a previously unexplored city. Walking the streets during the morning before a talk or workshop. Looking out of a plane or train window. Taking photographs. Sipping a glass of wine up at a bar. Enjoying a coffee sat at a table in a sunny square. Nosing in shop windows, daydreaming. That's when those creative sparks happen.

Doing those things, going somewhere new, observing, exploring – that's when I'm on fire. The tastes, sounds, sights come alive for me.

I'm so pleased I've continued my notepad habit these last 12 years or so. In the pages of my notebook collection I have observations, reflections and ideas from those journeys and places I've visited. When I flick through them again years later, I often find nuggets of inspiration and suggestions that are surprisingly timely. When this happens, it's the best – it's like your younger self giving your older self all the learnings you need.

And many of the ideas you are reading here started out in those notebooks.

107 Live in a 15-minute neighbourhood

I live in a town where most things we need are on our doorstep. The railway station, beach, schools, doctors' surgery, pharmacy, park, library, cafés, restaurants and shops are within a 15-minute walk. As well as the amenities within a 15-minute bike ride, there's also a vast woodland and a concert venue. I enjoy and appreciate having these things on my doorstep.

The concept of the 15-minute city is that of academic and scientist Carlos Moreno. A city, he says, needs to achieve six key functions – living, working, supplying, caring, learning and enjoying. Ensuring you can access everything close-by reduces the need for air-polluting travel. Moreno believes structuring our urban spaces in this way, where the emphasis is on localization, enhances our quality of life. I agree.

108 Focus on quality – not quantity – of hours

Thinking is hard, the Do Lectures and Hiut Denim co-founder David Hieatt told me, but scrolling is easy.

We can easily spend hours scrolling on our phones, but how to get focused on the work that matters? David thinks that most people have it the wrong way round – we obsess about managing our time, whereas we should really be focusing on managing our energy, how to get in the optimum state.

David told me he aims to get the important stuff done in two hours in the morning, when he's working alone on his farm. And then when his energy wanes he'll walk down the hill to the Hiut Denim factory and spend the afternoon with his team.

David's always looking at quality – not quantity – of hours.

109 Build up the energy

Whenever Nick and I spend time together – on a walk, for a coffee, or just on a call – he consistently gives me energy. So it's no surprise that what Nick needs in order to have a good day involves a boost of energy.

Nick spends his time between an office in Copenhagen and home in London. As we walked through Regent's Park, Nick told me a good day is where he's both consciously managing his own energy as well as being able to build up energy with those around him. How does he do that? By being intentional in finding the good on even the challenging days – and he usually finds that through seeking out positive people.

It's no coincidence we're discussing this on a walk through the park. Nick says that light exercise and movement make a huge difference to his day. When he can he steps away from his desk and joins a meeting on his headphones while walking around the park.

It's no wonder then that Nick is global head of talent at Ørsted – an energy company!

110 Let's have better bosses

Once upon a time I used to run a radio studio and production business. I have learned a lot about people and relationships since. Sometimes I wonder what I'd do differently as managing director if I led that team today. Here are five things I'd do to be a better boss:

1. Encourage people to get out of the office during the day.

2. Walk around the building more to be more visible and available.

3. Gather the team out of the office to get to know each other.

4. Ask how they are and, when they're not OK, work out ways to help.

5. Listen.

If you lead a team, how could you be a better leader? If you're not the boss, what do you need in order to flourish at work?

111 Talk to your plane neighbour

I was on an overnight flight from JFK to Heathrow. Just before take-off a nervous flyer asked to switch seats. At the last minute I found myself in a two-seat configuration next to a woman from New York. It was a fortuitous move. We got talking and spent the next few hours drinking red wine, deconstructing the episodes of the HBO series *Girls* that we watched on the screens in front of us. Later as the cabin lights dimmed, we hit the overhead light switch, sweet-talked the cabin crew for more wine, and kept chatting.

There is something quite life affirming in how two people, who've not met before, can go from introductory handshake to sharing a joke to discovering they're on the same wavelength. And then you never see them again.

It's about living in the moment in its richest sense, free in the knowledge that it is temporary, only for the here and now, where neither party asks, or is concerned with, what comes next.

112 Deal with your unsorted baggage

I've learned this the hard way – if you don't deal with your problems and struggles of the past, they'll catch up with you. Most of us will have a need to deal with what Bruce Springsteen describes – in his 2016 autobiography *Born To Run* – as our 'unsorted baggage': if you hide it away and ignore it, it will always be there, weighing you down.

I'm fortunate I found a good therapist who I feel was designed for me. She could see what made me tick. She could see the teenage me. She could see the professional me. She helped me unpack all my luggage, sort through it and discard what was no longer useful.

At the end of one particular therapy session, I broke the rules. As I was leaving she told me 'Don't give up,' and I gave her a hug. 'I needed to hear that today,' I said, as tears filled my eyes.

Sometimes you don't even think there's anything there to be dealt with, but having someone to talk it through can lift the weight you're unconsciously lugging about.

113 Don't be efficient

I used to run day-long workshops around the UK for journalists. The most efficient model for a freelancer like me would be to arrive the night before and then head home as soon as the workshop ends.

That way you maximize your billable days. But that's not what I'm after. As you know, I'm not about monetizing every fragment of my working week.

On a trip to Belfast I'm glad I didn't have a taxi waiting to take me to the airport. Once my workshop finished I had nowhere to rush off to, so when one of my delegates, Seamus, asked me if I wanted to see the real Belfast, I couldn't get in his car quick enough.

It was a drive-by history lesson that condensed 40 years into one hour. Seamus, a renowned veteran journalist who began his reporting career in Belfast in 1988, showed me the Falls Road, the Shankill Road, the Peace Line. It was an eye-opening experience I would have missed out on had I dashed off home.

Efficiency isn't always the right metric. Instead, making time to explore enabled me to see the real heart of Belfast, for which I'm ever grateful to Seamus.

114 Send a handwritten note

Yesterday I received a handwritten note from Aimee in Seattle. Last week I sent a postcard to Bree in New York. Today I'm sending a card to Claire and Sarah in Nottingham.

Isn't it lovely to receive a handwritten note or card in the post? And you never know where it might lead.

When I read *Reboot: Leadership and the Art of Growing Up* by Jerry Colonna, it really touched me. I was so taken with the book that straight after finishing it I wrote a snail-mail letter to Jerry in Boulder, Colorado. As a result, Jerry and I had a number of conversations on Twitter. That progressed to email, which led to us meeting in London when I hosted a fireside chat with him. And it sparked a relationship that continues to this day.

115 Go to an English village festival

One summer we were on holiday in Suffolk, driving through the country roads heading for the coast. As we approached the small village of Peasenhall we noticed hand-painted signs dotted along the street announcing 'The Peasenhall Pea Festival'.

A pea festival? It was just too intriguing. We had to take a look.

'This way peas,' said the sign in black Sharpie on cardboard as we worked out where to park.

When we got to the village hall, everything was themed around peas. I mean everything. Pea-flavoured ice cream. Sweet-pea cupcakes. A pea-eating competition. The World Pea Podding Championships. In the tombola, all the items were green.

We'd never been to anything like it. It was both hilarious, and also an incredible feat of ingenuity and organization – all from the committed residents of a tiny English village. To this day the memory of it continues to bring a smile to our faces.

116 Shop local. Shop independent

We have Andy, Sam, Phoebe and Simon in our favourite coffee shops. There's another Simon who's the greengrocer. Debbie and Linda in the card shop. Viv in the hardware store. Dave owns a skateshop. Jim's the butcher.

I'm lucky to live in a neighbourhood where we have lots of independent stores, where we know the traders and owners by name. I've got nothing against big retailers, but I find I'm much more likely to start chatting with the person behind the counter in an independent store.

It gets you knowing the people behind the business, building relationships, seeing their challenges, staying with them for the journey, and when you buy from these people you know the money is going back into the local economy.

Okay, shopping locally may cost more than going online. But when you get the personal touch, it's worth it. It's like a local tax. Pay a bit more to keep your neighbourhood thriving, and we all win.

117 Travel via food

When she was in her 20s, my wife Zoë lived in Japan for a year or so. It was an experience that has always stayed with her. She loved the country and the people and remembers her time there fondly.

The other weekend, Zoë and our two teenage boys made sushi at home. They took out the sushi mat and all the ingredients they needed, then added in fresh salmon from the fishmonger. And got rolling!

Zoë said that making sushi took her right back to Zushi (surely the perfect place for a sushi lover called Zoë?), a town in Kanagawa Prefecture, where she used to teach English. And this time we all got to join in. Luckily the kit made plenty of maki rolls and nigari, so she was happy to share.

118 Give Gogo the rabbit some water

After landing at Madrid's Barajas airport on a work trip, a fellow traveller – and complete stranger – beckoned me over. Could I help her?

She was trying to give her pet rabbit some water. The rabbit – who she explained was called Gogo – had just taken his first flight from London to Madrid, and was now heading to Lisbon. She was worried he was dehydrated. Could I give him some water through a pipette while she held him? Sure, I replied confidently. Then after five minutes, we had to give up. Who knew it could be so tricky!? The little rabbit firmly shut his jaw – he didn't want me squirting anything in his mouth.

I guess what I loved about it was that I was being helpful while also doing something unusual. When was the last time I watered a rabbit… at an international airport? A weird and wonderful encounter.

And I must admit, that was a strange text message my wife received from me afterwards!

119 Act on impulse

It was lunchtime in April in 2010. Walking up Wardour Street in Soho I thought the guy I'd just walked past looked familiar.

When I reached the sandwich shop, I tweeted that I thought I'd just seen @davestewart, the famous singer-songwriter and creative entrepreneur who is one half of the Eurythmics. Dave tweeted me back that he was stuck in London because of the Icelandic volcano that had closed European airspace. That started a conversation and the next month – when Dave was back in London – we met one Sunday afternoon at The Soho Hotel.

For some time before this meeting I'd had Dave on a list of inspiring people I'd wanted to meet and interview for my blog. I'd reached out to his office in LA but hadn't got anywhere. But this fortuitous spotting of Dave, who only happened to be in town because of an erupting volcano (bizarre, right?) spurred me to action. I'd acted on an impulse, and the stars aligned to make it happen.

Sweet Dreams are made of this? I'd say so!

120 Notice what you enjoy

I'm fascinated by the stories behind people starting their business.

Story number one. Since they opened their roastery on Redchurch Street in east London I've been a fan of Allpress Coffee. In the mid-1980s Michael Allpress went travelling from his native New Zealand and, in Seattle, he fell in love with the coffee scene. He returned home, and in 1989 opened Allpress Espresso Coffee Cart in Victoria Park in Auckland. His company has since expanded all over the world.

Story number two. Six years ago Andy was a heating engineer. Back then he wasn't interested in coffee. Then one day he went to a tattoo convention and tasted his first flat white. He fell in love with it. At the time he used to get his beard trimmed at a barbers on Redchurch Street. Nearby is Allpress, and on each visit Andy would pop in for his coffee fix. Over time, he got curious and knowledgeable about coffee and how it's roasted. Before long, he'd set his sights on opening his own coffee shop. I'm glad he did. Cult Coffee & Tattoos is the coffee shop at the top of my road. It's where Andy made me the Long Black I'm drinking right now.

CHAPTER 5

HEAD TOWARDS WHAT MAGNETIZES YOU

121 Reframe the story you tell yourself

Beware the story that you tell yourself – and those around you – of your life.

For too long I had my story wrong.

I was telling the 'I have struggled' story. Not the 'I survived' story.

I was telling the 'I had to quit my job' story. Not the 'look what I built' story.

I was telling the 'I don't earn as much money as I used to' story. Rather than the 'just look at the freedom I have' story.

I'm not erasing what happened, I'm reframing the lessons I'm taking from it all.

Sometimes we need to stop, reassess and see the positives. Start celebrating the adventure, rather than wallowing in the what-could-have-beens, in the regrets and frustrations. You've made it to here. You've succeeded so far, one way or another. It's taken resilience, faith, ingenuity, luck, poor decisions, good decisions.

Change your story and it will change your outlook. And if you change your outlook you may well change your fortunes.

True story ;)

122 Climb on the happy bus

The number 26 bus pulled up outside St Paul's Cathedral.

I got on board and flashed my Oyster card against the sensor by the driver's cabin.

'Good afternoon, how are you?' said the driver.

I paused then smiled and replied, 'Good thanks!'

I ran up to the top deck with a brand new spring in my step.

And as I looked around me, it felt like the driver's happy greeting was infectious, people smiled at each other.

A happy bus driver makes a happy bus.

Ding ding!

123 Stop, look and write down what you see

This is what I spotted yesterday walking through the city:

- A slightly rickety looking spiral staircase fire exit

- The weathered stone walls of an old church nestled between two modern office blocks

- A tree waving its leafy branches against the backdrop of a cloudless sky

- A woman hurrying along wearing a stripey top

- Two twenty-something men holding hands, heads tilted towards one another

- A receipt from a florist fluttering in the gutter.

When you lead a busy life it's easy to walk around with your head down, focused on your next appointment or looking down at your phone. When I realize I'm doing that I often challenge myself to stop, look up and around, and take out my notepad to jot down what I see. Just for a couple of minutes or so, I'll take in what's going on around me.

What interesting things are right there under your nose, when you just stop to look?

124 Step away from the desk

A rectangular surface on legs, usually grey or beige. Comes with a chair. Often black and swivels. Someone long ago decreed that sitting at a desk was where your work should be done. But that's just plain crazy if you think about it. Why on earth would you do your best, most creative, innovative, exciting and disruptive work sitting at an oblong piece of furniture?

Many of us do in fact have flexibility in our working day. We can move around the office building. We can switch a catch-up with someone to a walk and talk outside. We can have a meeting in the café on the corner.

You can't just plonk a human being anywhere and expect them to do their best work. Step away from the desk!

125 Head towards what magnetizes you

I learned the hard way. When I headed away from my passions, my story and my purpose – I became drained, dragged down and depleted.

The projects, roles and gigs where I had a spring in my step? These were the ones where I could be me – where I could bring all of my passions, beliefs and values to my work.

Amen to that! What gets you excited should act as a magnet, pulling you towards your true calling and purpose on this planet.

I work with a lot of individuals and organizations where my work's about encouraging them to stick to their guns, to stay aligned to their vision and not dilute who they really are. Their confidence is reignited and they have the fuel to keep going.

So whether you're a student, an executive looking for a career change or the founder of a growing business, my advice is always this: identify what magnetizes you, and head towards it.

126 Turn the dial from the usual

One Sunday morning we tuned into BBC World Service radio. In the 60 minutes that followed, I learned about the German elections, heard a wonderful audio essay by a woman in Damascus on ten years of conflict in Syria, and listened to a preview of Turkish author Elif Shafak's new book.

Spotify, podcasts, playlists. A favourite daily radio show. You choose where you put your attention.

But if you turn the dial from the usual you'll open your ears to something that stretches your mind and carries you away. Who knows what you'll learn or where you'll end up?

127 Have some plants in your office

The best office I've ever worked in? Second Home: a co-working space with sites in London, Los Angeles and Lisbon. The work of Spanish architects José Selgas and Lucía Cano. The spaces are bright, light and feature plants everywhere. They look stunning!

Second Home takes office plants to another level where it's more like a jungle. The Lisbon space has over 1,200 pot plants and trees among the desks.

Even when I worked in the east London Second Home for a few dull days one February it was still really cheery. Every internal wall is glass so there's lots of natural light too. The space bursts in colour and greenery, providing a healthy and interesting workspace.

So if you can't go and sample Second Home, perhaps consider how you can lift up the environment where you work, whether that's plants, or colourful boxes.

How can you make a visual difference to your space?

128 Think outside the job spec

Some of my best experiences in the world of work have been when I didn't feel boxed in by a job title, where I could experiment and improvise.

During a stint at a broadcasting company in the early 1990s, we were all flexible enough to roll up our sleeves and help a colleague out. So when a producer colleague asked me to step in for him and do some interviews for a radio show, I might have said *that's not my job* or that I didn't have the experience. I wasn't a radio producer or journalist. My only experience doing interviews had been six years earlier when I worked in radio as a teenager. But I said yes. Which is how I found myself in a suite at The Halkin hotel at a press junket interviewing Christian Slater and Patricia Arquette. And that wasn't in my job spec.

129 Find somewhere your lizard brain can relax

Last year Hugh Garry lived in Ibiza for three months. On the mornings he didn't go for a run, he told me he'd get up early, take a flask of tea and head down to the beach. He'd just sit there watching the sun come up.

Looking at the horizon, Hugh said, had a really calming effect on him.

Thinking about why it had been such a relaxing experience, he wondered whether it was because your lizard brain can switch off. The lizard brain is that primal part of your mind that is prepped to look for danger. It's a leftover from when we had to be on alert for sabre-toothed tigers. When you look at the horizon, Hugh thinks your lizard brain registers there are no dark corners where anything can hide; you can see far and wide that there are no predators coming to get you.

Find a beach or a field or a landscape to relax into and be truly at ease.

130 Talk to the cleaner

I was running a day-long workshop at the MediaCity office development in Salford. When I came out for lunch, I smiled at a guy who was wheeling his rubbish cart. We got chatting. His name was Sonny, he was a cleaning supervisor. Talking to him really lifted me – I had a spring in my step when I returned to inspire my delegates.

Behavioural science researchers at the University of Chicago ran a series of experiments where some commuters were asked to talk to a stranger on their journey to work, and some weren't. Reporting back how it felt, those who talked to strangers were the happiest following their commutes. Thanks to the release of a feel-good chemical in the brain called dopamine, you get a greater surge of pleasure from chance encounters than planned ones.

But with Sonny, I think there's something else in the encounter. Getting a perspective on life from someone who does such a vital job, but isn't often seen for who they are. So thank you Sonny, for bringing the sunshine.

131 Play with sticky notes

I love a sticky Post-it Note.

A Post-it Note signals something to me: a work-in-progress, a creative process, ideas being generated.

When I'm in complex-project-mode I put sticky notes all over my cork wall. They only stay up for a few weeks but I love that notion of having ideas, sticking them up on the wall, mixing them up, constantly being able to move around. A Post-it Note might have a silly idea on it, it might be screwed up and chucked away, but that's the beauty of them. It's a key part of the creative process. And the more day-glow the sticky note, the better.

132 Find your perfect city park

In Lisbon we discovered a beautiful little town park, Jardim do Príncipe Real. A 100-year-old cypress tree stretches out its octopus branches, now held up by a network of struts. There's a café and children's playground. Sunshine, trees and blossom. On the street corner is one of the little kiosks that are sprinkled throughout the city where you can get a perfect espresso for not very much.

Discovering Jardim do Príncipe Real was a present. It provided us with the perfect ingredients. The things I value. The things that really matter.

So it called us back. At 7pm we returned to the kiosk at the other corner of the park for a drink before dinner. People sitting in the late sun, in their suits, chatting and sipping beers.

I was magnetized by that little park. Just writing about it now makes me smile.

I feel I could come here every day and it would be enough.

133 Go to a library

In the Japanese city of Musashino is Musashino Place. It's a library and community centre designed by Yasuko Kawaharada and Takehiko Higa. The designers had a vision for a space that welcomes everyone. There are dance and craft spaces for teenagers, as well as lounge areas and a study room. Ceilings arch over light and airy space. It's populated with stylish wooden furniture.

Libraries are generally much more simple affairs. They are hushed and often unglamourous surroundings, where books line the rows waiting to be picked. Regardless, libraries are the lifeblood of a community. Even in this digital age, they are depositories of not only knowledge but imagination, other worlds, flights of fancy. They inspire and prod curiosity, they can stir creativity and take you to other countries. Often, they are oases of peace.

One day I'd love to get to Musashino. Until then I'll visit and nurture our local library, and help keep the beating heart pumping.

134 Slow beats fast

On the face of it the train was the least efficient route. But I love a journey so, when I last went to Edinburgh, I flew up but returned on the train. I found the trip back productive and energizing. Getting settled into my seat, I ordered a glass of red wine and hit play on the episode of *Desert Island Discs* (the guest was Tracey Thorn, in case you were wondering), looking out to the rolling waves of the North Sea.

It felt a million miles from a busy short-haul flight.

What's more, that changing landscape out of the train window triggered my creativity. Heading south, the view from my seat was like an ever-changing slide show: the North Sea coast; crossing the Tyne in Newcastle; and all the fields, hills, towns and villages that rolled out before me in between Edinburgh and London.

Go slow. Take it all in.

135 Find your magic chair

Janko told me there is a chair in one of the spaces he often works in that looks pretty ordinary. It's not designer or upholstered in a flash fabric, neither is it luxurious or quirky. But for Janko, it's love at first seat.

Why? Because it's right for him. When he sits down with his laptop his arms are at the right height for the keyboard. His posture is good. It's comfortable. He always does good work there.

And because he always does good work there, he keeps going back to it.

And because he keeps going back to it, he keeps doing good work.

(Get it?)

Do you have a favourite chair or couch in your home or office that gives your creativity and productivity an edge?

136 Order some Lego for the office

When I arrived at my very first South by South West conference and walked into the Austin Convention Center, I was met with the largest pile of Lego I had ever seen. And on a long shelf by the ground to ceiling windows, were the most elaborate and sophisticated Lego models and constructions you could ever imagine.

Whenever I walked past it over the next few days, the Lego pit was busy with delegates sitting childlike, brows furrowed in concentration as they burrowed through the mountain of coloured rectangles trying to find the right piece.

It made me think that every office building should have Lego. Somewhere to play with ideas. To have a moment of calm. To collaborate. Or just to get lost among the coloured bricks.

137 Create blank space

I once worked with executives at a fintech company in London whose calendars looked like a game of Tetris – back to back meetings with no space for thinking. One member of the team told me she only had space for ideas when she was on a business trip.

Especially for those of us who have roles that require creative thinking – innovating, coming up with ideas, solving problems – how can you get better at creating blank space in your day?

New York-based author Kelly Hoey – who we first met in Idea #98 – told me she tried an experiment when she was writing her book *Build Your Dream Network*. She'd keep mornings free so she could write – she knew that was when she was at her best. When the events of 2020 hit, she spent more and more time on calls at her desk in her midtown apartment. She knew she had to carve out time to think about and plan new projects and started a new regime: no meetings or calls on a Monday or a Friday. It's worked so well, she's kept it going. She told me doing that had created many more good days for her.

138 Go the extra mile

When I decided to arrange an event about storytelling in my hometown, I thought the room would be full of locals. But then there was Nick, who'd come all the way from Cardiff on the other side of the UK. He'd travelled by train and his fold-up bike.

When I hosted a day-long workshop in London and we went around the room asking where everybody was from, I was surprised to hear Terin say she'd flown in specially from New York.

When you go the extra mile – put in extraordinary effort – to attend an event, it sends a signal of how committed you are. You are not only curious about learning, you're happy to jump on a bike or plane to get there. It's a mindset that gives it your all.

And knowing Nick and Terin had travelled so far put the pressure on me. I thought I'd better give 110 per cent to make sure these were really great gigs!

139 Open a passion shop

I've met many entrepreneurs who've made a success of starting a business built on their passions.

Of course, entrepreneurship and retail can be really tough. But if you're so passionate about what you're selling – that can give you the rocket fuel you need.

CW Pencils on New York's Lower East Side sells – you guessed it – pencils. Pencils from as far afield as India, and as near as Jersey City. When I visited the store 12 months after opening, founder Caroline Weaver – a life-long pencil lover and collector – told me that while she always had a passion for pencils, she admitted she wasn't sure how popular her store would be. But it's still going strong today.

I know entrepreneurship is hard. So if you're starting a business, it's got to be something you're passionate about, and you'll communicate your love of what you do to others, even with a niche product.

140 Take a feather out of Mr Bird's cap

Dickie Bird is a famous English cricket umpire who spent 12 months across 2020–21 shielding at his Yorkshire home alone. He knew he couldn't stay inside all day looking at the four walls so he started a daily exercise routine.

He told a BBC interviewer that every day he'd spend an hour exercising outside, running up and down his garden or running on the spot. And then he'd take a 1½-hour walk along the country roads.

He said it made him feel really good. He's 88.

141 Put some art on the wall

On the face of it, it wasn't that remarkable.

A photograph in a magazine of five discarded watermelon slices in a stainless steel sink. For some reason, I loved it. The red segments against the silver of the stainless steel. The droplets of water in the sink. The well-worn wooden worktop.

I tracked down the photographer Federico, who is based in Milan, and asked if he would sell me a print. And now it's in a frame on my wall.

Whether it's a print or a postcard from an exhibition, art on the walls never fails to cheer me up. On my pinboard I've got one of my favourite photographs. And it only cost me the price of a newspaper: a clipping of Jeff Mermelstein's 'Sidewalk' – a photograph of a man on a New York street with a paperback in his mouth.

It doesn't need a big investment, other than your love for it.

142 Express yourself

In one photograph she's standing by her bookshelf in a cashmere cardigan. In another she's on her doorstep in a long dress and chunky necklace. And then there's one of her in the garden wearing a skirt made from material purchased at Lekki Market in Lagos, Nigeria. This is my friend Gillian Licari on Instagram, where she is @gettingoninstyle.

Gillian – a Canadian in London who used to work at Canada House in Trafalgar Square – launched her Instagram account as she was about to retire from full-time work. Just because she no longer went to an office didn't mean she was going to give up on her style. Gillian challenges herself each day to wear an outfit that makes her feel good. And she posts those outfits on her Instagram, along with the hashtag #fashionover60.

Gillian has friends spread far and wide, some of whom she doesn't see much, so her social media account is a great way to connect, while demonstrating her love of clothes. Gillian says that getting great feedback makes for a great day.

143 Walk to power your day

It's free, for most of us it's easy to do, and you can go any which way you choose once you step out of the office or your front door. If there is ever one thing I evangelize more than anything else, it's going for a walk. Even five minutes can make a difference to your quality of day. Stretch your legs to:

1. Take in your surroundings and see what thoughts it prompts

2. Have a more productive meeting

3. Take a break when you're feeling stressed

4. Move around to get the creative juices flowing

5. Grab a friend or colleague to work through a challenge together.

144 Know what you're fighting for

My work friend Lizzie Everard told me a question she'd been asking: 'What is it that you're fighting for?'

It's smart, because it takes 'What are you passionate about?' to another level.

'What are you fighting for?' It's galvanizing. What stirs you to action, what causes do you champion, what gets you ploughing through each day to make a difference?

Me?

I'm fighting for freedom. For independence. For not being shackled.

For not having to go to an office every day. For not having to be someone I'm not.

For not having to fake it.

How about you? What puts a fire in your belly? It might be one overarching concept that propels you to get up each day and make a difference, and guide your efforts towards what's important.

145 Take your time climbing the mountain

Anything worthwhile takes a long time, says Debbie Millman, host of the Design Matters podcast.

In 2019, Debbie featured music legend David Lee Roth on her podcast. David was lead-singer of the band Van Halen, perhaps best known for their hit 'Jump'. Debbie asked David how it felt in 1984 when his band was at the top of their game.

David replied that you should think carefully about getting to the top of the tallest mountain because, he says, you're most likely to be alone, it will be freezing cold and there is only one direction to go next!

So often you can rush to climb to the peak of your career. You want to race through to tick off your ambitions and goals. I love David's cautionary tale – that if you peak too early, then where does that leave you?

146 Subtract don't add

I read an article in The Economist about a paper published in the academic journal Nature. The paper explains a human tendency which is quite intriguing. It found that when people were asked to improve something – a golf course, a Lego model, or a report they're writing – they tended to think about adding something to the item. They were less likely to immediately think of subtracting something, even when taking something away was the better solution.

It suggests this is why people struggle to improve things ranging from organizational red tape to their overburdened schedules at work.

So if you want to improve anything in your life – your surroundings, your schedule, even how you live your life – could the answer be about taking away, not adding?

147 Take your kid for an impromptu trip to the ice-cream parlour

Isn't it often the way that spontaneous experiences trump planned ones?

Having a last-minute takeaway curry on a Friday night might feel more of a treat than if you'd planned it.

I can remember one such impromptu moment with my eldest son. I'd gone out in the car to pick him up and when we got home I couldn't find a parking space on our street. So after driving around the block with no success, I said to him – let's drive to Rossi!

A spur of the moment trip to our local town's historic ice cream parlour. We sat in the window at a formica table, looking out at the sea, having a chat about his school day. Just the two of us. Totally unplanned. What a special moment.

I'm glad there were no parking spaces.

148 Head out on the stoop

It had been a wet, grey day. Persistent rain falling on Amsterdam's cobbled streets and canals.

And then at 4.45pm there was that wonderful moment when it all changed. The clouds cleared, the sun shone, the light glinting off the shiny wet cobblestones. And as it did so, Amsterdammers came out of their houses and apartments and onto their stoops. Bringing chairs and stools outside.

I sat on a bench and watched.

Two elderly ladies carrying a tray of two glasses of red wine.

A fifty-something woman with a beer and a paperback.

A woman with a bowl of pasta.

A family, the granddad with a bottle of wine in the crook of his arm, holding a board of cheese.

Late afternoon out on the stoop.

I love that sense of making the most of it. Of soaking up the sun, and enjoying life's pleasures on your doorstep. Taking your home outside.

149 Make your other half cry with laughter

On the day-long workshops I used to run around the UK, I often gave the delegates a break during the afternoon.

What did I do during that break? Sometimes I walked outside to stretch my legs and get some fresh air. But other times I would just video-call my wife and make her laugh. Like make her really laugh – cry with laughter.

I don't know why I did it. I'd see her that night or the next day, but there was something mischievous about doing something totally silly, messing around before the delegates returned for the next session.

150 Give someone a flower-flash!

Back in November 2020, if you'd walked past the boarded up Brooks Brothers store on the corner of 20th and Broadway in New York City, you'd have seen something unusual emerging from the trash can on the street corner.

A riot of colour in the form of a six-foot display of roses, asters, delphiniums and sugar maple spilling out high and wide.

It was the work of florist Lewis Miller – what he calls a flower-flash. A concept born one evening when Miller was leaving his studio with an armload of leftover flowers. Miller does it because he loves the ability of flowers to light people up.

I love that spirit. Imagine the impact on passers-by. And I wonder how you can give someone an equivalent of a flower-flash. A WhatsApp sending a photograph of a shared memory? Surprising your partner with a piece of cake from their favourite patisserie? A handwritten note?

CHAPTER 6
TOP UP YOUR FUEL TANK

151 Choose to be kind

Whether you're giving up your seat to someone who needs it on the subway, letting someone with only a couple of items go ahead of you in the supermarket queue, or reaching something down for an elderly person off the top shelf – the choice is yours: whether to be kind or unkind.

And when you're kind, it gives you a boost too.

A review of decades of research on the effects of kindness, published by the American Psychological Association, discovered that doing small, occasional acts of kindness can make you happier than doing formal acts of kindness, like volunteering for a charity.

People who were kind often had higher self-esteem and had a keener sense of their own capabilities. Reasons why kindness might give us a boost? It's suggested it socially connects us, gives us a warm feeling and provides our life with meaning.

152 It's never too late to try something different

At the beginning of 2003, I was 35. Newly single. Self-employed. I didn't have much work going on. I had the opportunity to do something life-changing. Rent out my house and go and stay with a friend in NYC and try my hand at something new. Go travelling. Go write a novel.

But I did none of those things.

Do you know why?

Because at the time I thought I was too old.

35! Thirty-f***ing-five!

Now when I look back at that from my 50s, I wonder why I thought that. And when I'm 80, I don't want to look back and think – whoa, you were only 55 and you thought you were too old.

Really, it's never too late to embrace trying something completely different.

153 Make sure your teenage self is present

A designer called James came on one of my Fuel Safaris – the walking sessions I run where I help people redesign their work lives. What struck me was how he'd succeeded putting his teenage spirit centre-stage in his work life as an adult. That strong creative and independent outlook he had as a 14-year-old – going out with his mates on their bikes, designing logos in his bedroom, the freedom to work when and where he fancies – is at the heart of who he is as a 30-year-old today.

Your young spirit often gets quashed when you're older. You think you have to grow up and be serious. Injecting a sliver of your younger self – whether that's your adventurous spirit or a desire to go against the flow – can give you the confidence boost you need. Bringing you creativity, energy and success.

I can honestly say that when the teenage archetype isn't present in my life today, I don't walk so tall. I don't feel I'm standing in the spot where I'm meant to be standing.

It's my secret sauce.

154 Top up your fuel tank

Stopping to refuel is part of any long journey and if you ignore that red indicator light, you'll be breaking down by the side of the road before too long.

We get the importance of filling up our fuel tanks. Yet do you pay the same attention to the low gauge in your own life?

And are you alert to when your needle sinks to zero, or do you carry on, convincing yourself you'll be fine?

You ignore those signs at your peril. Think about how you can refuel. What do you need in order to live your best life, and ensure you aren't tackling your days on an empty tank? Is it exercise, taking a break, getting an early night?

Top up your tank before you're languishing on the verge, spent of energy.

155 Share your life stories at work

Humans have shared stories for thousands of years. Seated around the campfire our ancestors shared stories to pass on knowledge and information, to connect their communities.

When you hear a story you care about, oxytocin is generated, the chemical associated with empathy.

One November evening in a country hotel in Kent, I hosted a company awayday. We ended the day in a Jacobean library. Around the crackling fire I asked the team to share their personal stories of 'how they got to here'. The honesty and emotion that tumbled out was humbling and inspiring. Through the telling of the stories, each of us could see we're all the same – same worries, same wishes, same challenges. The people in the room bonded through their stories and left a lasting impact beyond that awayday. Telling these personal stories created an environment of openness, equality and trust.

Magic happens when you open up and share your story.

156 Look at the world outside your office

Tinker Hatfield is vice president for design and special projects at Nike, responsible for innovation. In the Netflix documentary *Abstract*, he explains that getting out and experiencing life gives you a library in your head. Far from seeing the world around you as a distraction, Tinker sees it a necessity to provide you with ideas, clarity and energy. The thoughts and concepts you pick up will translate into new ideas.

When you lead a busy work life it's easy to see what's going on 'over there', outside of your immediate sphere, as a nuisance or interference. But taking a leaf out of Tinker's book, it could be viewed instead as a source of inspiration. Local parks and squares, the bookstore around the corner. There's often so much right on your doorstep, yet it's so easy to overlook what's right in front of you.

157 Show your appreciation with *kolay gelsin*

When you're walking past a street cleaner, a garbage truck or a hospital porter, you might want to show your appreciation. Especially where you know the person doing the job is likely to be poorly paid, ignored or under-appreciated.

The Turkish have an expression that's perfect for these occasions.

Kolay gelsin.

It means 'Keep up the good work'.

Whether it's your delivery driver or a housekeeper in a hotel, let's keep *kolay gelsin* in mind and show your appreciation to those that deserve it.

158 Take a stranger to a bar

My friend Claire is a journalist in New York. She travels a lot for her job and enjoys the random encounters with strangers that happen along the way.

'What is it,' I asked her, 'that you like about talking to strangers?' It's her natural curiosity, she says. She's simply interested in other people's stories.

Claire told me the time she once boarded a plane and found herself in a row of three seats alongside a Hollywood make-up artist and an aspiring musician. The plane was delayed so they shared their snacks, ordered some wine and had a great time – all while still stuck on the ground. Today they're all still in touch on Facebook.

On another occasion she was stranded in Ohio en route to a big interview. The flight had been delayed and she found herself next to a woman who had just come from a funeral. Claire decided to cheer her up by taking her to the bar in the airport, where they had a long moan about life's ups and downs.

The bar's name? The Stewing Pot.

159 Mindset beats tools

When it comes to staying organized, I find the right mindset beats having the right tools. Shiny apps and expensive software can be helpful of course. But often that's underpinned by having the right approach.

I've been running my own business for 21 years. But I have no small business software to run my financial side of the business. I have a bunch of spreadsheets and an invoicing template that I've been using for over a decade and it does the job. It's uncomplicated and straightforward. All it needs is for me to update it regularly and accurately. It's easy to interrogate and to spot mistakes. Better to be organized and across what needs to be done rather than seduced by a shiny app.

160 Make a stand

In many ways I was a typical 1980s teenager – passionate about supporting causes I believed in. I marched for the Anti-Apartheid Movement. I lay down in the street protesting against student loans. I went on a rally to raise awareness about a journalist taken hostage in Beirut. I wrote letters to newspapers about issues I cared about, I rang doorbells, I delivered flyers.

I'm glad I got involved. I felt I was part of something and that my efforts helped make a difference. Now we've got digital tools at our disposal, it's easier than ever to make a stand. We can lobby lawmakers. Protest against unethical brands. Sign online petitions. Blow the whistle on toxic workplaces, bullying bosses, racial injustice or sexual discrimination.

Part of having a good day is about recognizing your own position in the world, and what you can do to help others or be an ally to those who might not have the same privilege or advantages. Whether it's Black Lives Matter, #metoo or gender equality, we all have a role to play.

Don't be a fence sitter. Do something.

161 Get physical

Most of us know that regular physical exercise can improve your day.

It can have a positive impact on your mood, outlook and mental health. Physical activity helps you sleep better, releases feel-good hormones and produces cortisol, which helps you manage stress. And if you're worrying about something, physical exercise can transport you away from all that.

And the good news is you don't need to hike up a mountain or run a marathon.

Just do whatever you fancy. Walk. Run. Bike ride. Workout.

And if you're able to walk or cycle to work, so much the better. Participants at my 'More Good Days at Work' workshop who walk or cycle to work often speak of a stress-free commute – it also makes for a healthy punctuation mark between home and office.

162 Lose yourself in your work

There's a lovely moment in The War on Drugs' performance of 'Eyes To The Wind' on the TV show *Austin City Limits* – you can find it on YouTube – where drummer Charlie Hall is lost in his work.

That look on his face. Charlie's doing the work that matters. His dedication to the task he's been given, of playing drums on a track that he must have played live hundreds of times, jumps out the screen at you. He's giving it absolutely everything. He's giving himself over to his craft.

And when his colleague Jon Natchez comes in for the sax solo, the smile on Charlie's face tells us he's utterly in his element.

I've seen that look before. It could be on the face of a barista, or a cocktail mixer. She could be driving a truck, or a police officer on a street corner. And if you can achieve that feeling on a daily basis, that is a good place to be.

163 Give it a go!

One of the most enjoyable gigs I've had in my career was a stint writing about entrepreneurship for the *Financial Times*. My love of ideas, meeting new people and finding out their stories all came together here.

Buddhism has a concept of the 'beginner's mindset' where we clear our minds and approach a challenge or new horizon with no preconceptions. We apply a childlike curiosity to give something a go.

I guess that's my story writing for the FT. I got it because, in part, I was persistent in knocking on the door of the editor, finally persuading him to meet me for a coffee. I've never taken a journalism or writing course in my life. I pitched him an idea. He commissioned my first article. It got plaudits in the morning editorial conference and I was off.

It's a reminder that you don't need to be qualified or an expert to get a chance. My only qualification was my passion for ideas, and making it happen. I was the unashamed hungry beginner.

164 Stay in an Airbnb

When you stay in an Airbnb rather than a hotel, you get a unique experience. I remember staying at my first Airbnb in Amsterdam in 2013 with my wife and kids. It was in a neighbourhood called De Pijp. When we arrived the fridge was stocked with wine, meats and cheese. There was a huge vase of multi-coloured tulips on the table.

And when the host Ester, who lived upstairs, realized we had two young boys she went and fetched a plastic crate full of Playmobil.

Oh how they *loved* Playmobil. It was the best thing Ester could have found for them. They felt at home.

So we all had an especially good time, because of those small touches, because Ester really cared about our experience and created a fabulous home-from-home vibe. And we wouldn't have got that Playmobil in a hotel!

165 Take a leap and Go Ape!

For our eldest son's eighth birthday his treat was a Go Ape adventure high up in the trees in Thetford Forest. The four of us were tethered to safety ropes as we navigated Tarzan swings and zip wires. There was a rope-ladder bridge and a walkway with stepping stones. Everything swung wildly as soon as you put one foot on it. Our youngest was not quite six and could barely reach to hold on, so he hung onto me instead.

My face was fixed into a half-grimace, half-smile as I made my way around the course.

Yet there was one thing that was particularly enjoyable, and that was watching the birthday boy always out in front, completely fearless, nimbly dancing over the pathways in the air as we gingerly snail-paced behind him.

He's always had that spirit to get stuck in and go for it. So when I'm feeling nervous about a situation I remember my son in the treetops. I channel his inner 'ape' as I take a leap onto the metaphorical swinging bridge!

166 Present things beautifully

Whenever I make a salad for me and my wife, I cut up all the ingredients carefully and mix it all together in a large, decorative bowl, even if it's an otherwise mundane Monday lunchtime. It makes a difference to the meal.

The Japanese have a tradition of presenting things beautifully, such as with the segmented bento boxes and the intricate wrapping of items in a shop.

Putting in the effort to enhance the way something looks enhances the overall experience.

167 Glass half-full

Whether you have an optimistic or pessimistic worldview makes a big difference to your wellbeing.

If you read certain newspapers or news websites they want you to believe how awful things are.

I like to take a more optimistic view of fellow humankind.

This morning on my dog walk a man was collecting rubbish from beside an overflowing bin and putting it in a bag. I smiled and thanked him.

You could take the view how awful it is to drop litter. It is, I agree. But you could instead focus on the goodness of other people who spend their time clearing up.

Having a pessimistic worldview is draining. You end up looking for the negative and finding it. It can become a vicious circle. Putting a positive spin on things doesn't have a draining effect.

I find I'm more tuned in to spotting and celebrating those acts of kindness around me. And probably I'll feel more inclined to do more of them myself. Can you change the world by changing your view of it?

168 Go for a swim

Some days it's five minutes, other days 45.

Some days a brisk one at 8am, other days a relaxed 7pm one in the sunshine. Occasionally it's raining.

Sometimes it's so cold you don't want to be in for long, other times you never want to get out.

Last year I clocked up over 90 dips from my local beach, located at the bottom of the road. Okay, the water's not ocean blue, it's estuary green.

Seaweed swirls around the surface, mud squelches under feet. And in truth, I'm not a fantastic swimmer. But I love it every time, whatever the conditions.

I relish that first submersion, ploughing through the water. It makes me feel invincible. As I do so, all my stresses or worries disappear.

I'm in my element. It boosts me every single time.

169 There is always a first time

I'd never run a marketing agency when I got hired by Benetton to be their marketing agency.

I'd never taken a journalism class when I got commissioned to write for the *Financial Times*.

And I had no idea of how to make a living self-employed when I took the leap to go freelance.

There's always a first time. Take an opportunity when you spot it, even if you don't think you're ready. Say yes, and figure it out afterwards.

170 Know that anything is possible

Yinka Ilori – the artist famous for his brightly coloured furniture designs and street hoardings – posted a pair of photographs on Instagram. The first photograph was of a name badge from the time he worked on the tills at Marks & Spencer. The accompanying text said during that time he used to dream he'd become a full-time artist with his own team and studio.

In the second photograph is a huge billboard of his work from the present day. In large, colourful letters is the slogan: 'If you can dream then anything is possible.' Yinka achieved his dream. He worked at Marks & Spencer for six years yet kept focused on what he truly wanted.

Your dream might be a long shot, but having it is the first stage to making it happen.

171 Check in somewhere that makes you fly!

On a self-funded work trip to New York, I'd opted for a cheap tourist hotel to keep costs down. If only I'd realized before booking it how much of a miserable place it was. I had a sense of foreboding each time I walked through the doors. It filled me with melancholy every time I returned to my bedroom. Yeah, it was awful.

But what's the point of being in a wonderful city, and staying somewhere like that?

Enough was enough. Life's too short for crap hotels.

I checked out, and for the last two nights I checked into the Ace Hotel. When I arrived I walked through a lobby full of people who seemed more me (okay, way cooler than me). It had a vibe, it had a heart.

Yes, the room cost more money. In truth I'd gone over my budget but hell, could I feel the difference? It gave me more than a spring in my step, it made me FLY!

The cloud that had been hovering the first couple of days lifted and I felt reinvigorated, happier and instantly more productive.

172 Create your own moodboard

The wall above my desk is covered in cork tiles. It's a giant pinboard.

There are postcards from art galleries. Photographs of my wife and children. A ticket stub from a San Francisco tram. An invitation to a billionaire's party on a yacht at Cannes (c'mon – I wasn't going to throw that away!). A backstage pass for a Billy Bragg gig. Torn out photographs from magazines. Postcards from friends and strangers. Quotes I've heard. Nice things people have said about me. A photograph of my favourite hotel.

Surrounding myself with my own moodboard stimulates, fuels and feeds me daily.

173 Be fully-in

My friend Nick has a great one-liner on his LinkedIn profile, where you'd typically find the person's job title.

It reads, 'I don't do things by halves.'

That sounds very Nick – he brings his infectious energy and passion to everything he touches.

I believe that when you are all-in, and you bring your all to everything, you increase the chances of success. I aim to be fully-in, wholly committed, totally dedicated in all I do across my personal life, family life and professional life too.

174 Believe it!

When my kids were small, the most tangible part of my professional life was that I wrote books. They told their teacher, 'My dad is a writer.'

My youngest son often would ask to borrow a laptop or the iPad and, with no preparation, would crank out stories.

One day he asked if I could get his book published. He said he wanted to have it sold in a bookshop.

I explained it wasn't as easy as that. That it would be quite complex. He couldn't see that. He thought that because I'd authored books, he could too. It had normalized things for him. He didn't see being a published writer as a hard thing to pull off. He just assumed he could write and that he could get his books into bookshops.

Young kids' spirits are awesome. They don't have negative self-belief or put hurdles in their way.

How can you cultivate that sense again that anything is possible? Because in all likelihood it really is possible. Sometimes you need to stop and think like a kid again.

175 Practice, practice, practice

There's a time and a place for blagging it, winging it.

But if you want to deliver great work, you have to prepare. When you've done your preparation, you know your stuff. It gives you confidence. When I'm delivering a new workshop or a major presentation, a huge amount of work goes in beforehand to maximize success.

I don't leave it to fate. I certainly don't wing it on the day.

I have a comprehensive rehearsal ritual.

In my attic workspace I put my slides up on my monitor and walk around the room as if I was doing it in front of an audience.

I'll make notes on where I could improve it. I'll time myself to check the duration. I'll record it on my phone and listen back to review it.

Practice, practice, practice. There is no way around it.

If you know your material and have shaped the presentation or workshop to the minute, you are 99 per cent there.

176 Just hit 'upload'

One August a few years ago, I was picked up from my front door and driven to Heathrow for a flight to Munich. On arrival in Germany, I was collected in a top of the range BMW and dropped off at my hotel in Holzkirchen where I spent the night. The next morning I did what I'd come here to do – namely, run a little ideas session for a couple of business people I'd never met before.

How did that opportunity come about?

Because someone watched a video I'd posted on YouTube.

Now, I don't have many followers. I haven't created a proper page for my channel. I haven't thought about tags or descriptions. I just put some videos up there when I fancy it. There's no strategy.

And yet, the German gig only happened because the person who hired me watched a video I'd nearly forgotten about. Sometimes strategy is less important than doing good work and putting it out there. Who knows who it will attract?

177 Set up a pop-up advice booth in the park

Every Friday Matthew Stillman used to take the subway from his home in Harlem, New York, down to Union Square and set up a table, two chairs and a sign inviting people to come and discuss whatever's on their mind. He started the experiment after completing a course on how to think creatively.

Matthew did this for ten years, listening to thousands of New Yorkers that included a gang member on the run and a woman having an affair.

Over a New York coffee, Matthew told me that having spent an entire day sitting outside, everything feels slower. Just sitting there in Union

Square, counterintuitively to how we usually spend our days, he says, gave him almost a post-meditative, semi-hypnotic state. In the same way his presence was beneficial to others, it was beneficial to himself too.

As creative projects go, this was pretty intense, but it shows you how being there for others can help yourself too.

178 Reach out to your heroes

Since the early 1990s, I've been inspired by the fashion designer and entrepreneur Sir Paul Smith, not only for his enduring talent and approach to life, but because whenever I've read stories about him there's one thing that shines through – what a lovely guy he is.

A few years ago I sent him a handwritten letter, together with a little booklet I made.

A couple of days later his assistant emailed to invite me to a talk he was giving at London's Design Museum.

When I met him, I said you won't remember this, as I know you get sent so much stuff, but I sent you a card and a little booklet.

He said, 'Yeah I know – I saw it. That's why I asked my assistant to invite you tonight!'

Reach out to your heroes.

And Sir Paul, you're always a class act.

179 Embrace the kids' mess

When my kids were small, Playmobil would be strewn across the floor. Boats. Planes. Campervans. Small figures in helmets or holding fire hoses or knights on horseback. We'd been lucky, having had a lot of it handed down from my sister and her two older boys.

I loved their own little made-up world spread out across the ground floor of our house. But sometimes I wished it wasn't such a mess and that it could get tidied away.

And now they have become teenagers of course the Playmobil has been packed up – we've passed it on to two little kids down the street.

Note to self: don't wish that mess away too soon. I'd be happy to see it again.

180 Join a club

Why are people who live in Denmark so happy? According to a survey by Aalborg University, nine out of ten Danes are members of a *forening*, the Danish word for a club or association.

From winter-bathing to board games, it appears that teaming up with others to play or engage in a hobby keeps their happiness up. In a 2018 Eurobarometer survey, 79 per cent of Danes reported never or almost never being lonely.

CHAPTER 7

PLAY WHERE YOU PLAY BEST

181 Play where you play best

You probably have a sense of what you're good at and what you're not good at.

And I think in life we have better days when we play where we play best, rather than focus our energies on those things we aren't so good at.

Tiger Woods once said he spent 80 per cent of the time practising on making his strengths better, not his weaknesses.

I am always learning, trying new things and trying to get better at things that I need to. But I know my strengths. And I know what I'm not good at.

So if you asked me to help you create a business plan for your startup, I'd say no.

But if you wanted to hire me to inspire your team or to help your organization tell its story, it's a fat yes.

How about you?

182 Appreciate a teacher who gets you

At school there was only one teacher who understood me. His name was Mr Tilley. He taught me A Level Politics. It wasn't just his engaging teaching style, he showed an interest in me as an individual.

When he learned how much I loved music, he lent me some of his favourite albums – I'm indebted to him for opening my ears to Joni Mitchell's album *Blue*.

Mr Tilley saw me for who I was. Unlike other teachers, he didn't make any attempt to change me.

When my youngest son was ten years old we went to see his teacher Mr Halsall for an annual appointment. He told us how well he was doing.

And as we got up to leave the classroom he gave this parting advice to my son: 'Carry on being you.'

Thanks Mr Halsall. Music to my ears.

183 Leave your phones outside the bedroom door

As parents of two teenage sons, we have one rule when bedtime comes. Leave your phone outside the door.

Not bringing my phone into the bedroom was a game changer for me. When I used to leave it on my bedside table, it was too tempting not to check it one more time before I turned the light off. Then on waking, the very first thing I'd do was switch it on.

I didn't like how I was so wedded to my phone. It was dictating how I both ended and started my day. I no longer wanted to be beholden to it.

Now at bedtime my phone stays outside. And during the day I set a limit on the amount of time I spend on social media. Okay, sometimes when I hit my daily limit, I ignore it. But knowing there is a time limit – that I'd rather not hit – makes me think twice when reaching for my phone.

There is a time and a place for your phone. After all, they are great when you are in control. But when they seep into every area of life, you have to say enough is enough.

184 Get in your element

My local photographer friend, Paul Tait, told me a story about early in his career when he was hired for an assignment in New York. He made all the arrangements from London, booking the studio and equipment and hiring an assistant for the day. When he turned up he found it all quite overwhelming.

It was his first time working in New York in unfamiliar surroundings and with an unknown assistant. How would it all go? But then something changed. As soon as he picked up his camera and felt the familiarity of it in his hands he started to feel better. Once he looked through the lens, that was it: he was back in his element. In that instant he knew that everything would be okay.

185 Hit 'play' on your feel-good track

Music is a jump-start to your quality of life – often a quick hack to get you in the right mood or mindset.

So tune into that piece of music that gets you in a good mood.

I have a bunch of YouTube links guaranteed to give me rocket fuel:

August Greene's performance on NPR's 'Tiny Desk'

The Canadian community choir Choir Choir Choir singing The Smiths

Future Islands playing 'Seasons' on *David Letterman*

Or my current go-to clip: The War on Drugs 'Eyes To The Wind' from the band's performance on the TV show *Austin City Limits*. It never fails to lift me and put me in the right mood.

So if a song sings to you, put that needle on the record and listen again, again, again.

186 Write your daily goals on the calendar

David Sloly told me his son bought him a *National Geographic* calendar for Christmas. On each page David writes three columns: Riches, Wisdom, Strength.

And alongside each David writes what he's doing that day to advance him in those three areas. For Riches, it might be reorganizing his invoices. For Wisdom, it could be the online course he is taking. And for Strength, going for a run or lifting weights. He makes sure he can put something against each.

Each day he asks himself: what can I do today to become richer, wiser, stronger?

I wondered whether thinking about these three things every day felt pressured, but David said they're often small things so they never feel like a chore. Even lifting a dumbbell for 60 seconds, he says, is moving him forward, and he likes to feel like he is moving forward.

Which three columns could you put on your calendar? What activities would you do each day to advance your goal?

187 Have a to-don't list

As I've got older I've become more focused on where I put my attention.

That doesn't mean I stay too safe or comfortable. I'm still looking to expose myself to new experiences.

But I am clear about what I don't want to do.

And having a to-don't list can be just as empowering as a to-do list.

Not only for what you're doing but who you spend time with too.

No, I won't watch a two-and-a-half-hour action movie.

No, I won't spend time with people who drain me.

No, I don't want to hang out in the tourist district of a city.

Having a mental to-don't list by default keeps me focused on what I *do* want to do.

188 Make 'em laugh…

When I used to run workshops for journalists at the BBC, I liked to throw new elements into the line-up, both to shake things up for me and to make sure I was keeping the delegates engaged.

In March 2017, I was running a workshop in Cardiff. On my lunch break I saw Twitter going crazy for a clip that had just aired on BBC World News: a man being interviewed over Skype as he's interrupted by first his toddler dancing in, followed by his baby in a walker. I'm sure you know the one. It's pure gold.

I kicked off the afternoon session by showing the clip. The delegates roared with laughter! They asked to see it again.

Something changed in that room there and then. Daniel Coyle, in his book *The Culture Code*, explains that laughter is the most fundamental sign of safety and connection, helping us to build bonds, be more open and trust one another.

Since then, I always ensure there's a chance to laugh in my workshops.

189 Don't compare your insides with others' outsides

When it comes down to it, things on the inside are rarely as they appear on the outside. Perception is different from reality.

The startup entrepreneur who's killing it? She's actually struggling. Just like the rest of us.

The Instagram stars with immaculate kitchens and shiny lifestyles? Sometimes, they fake it too.

So you should stop beating yourself up, comparing yourself with others who, through the magic of social media, may appear to be having more 'successful' lives than ours. You don't know what's going on on the inside. You don't see the turmoil and angst.

Similarly in the offline world. You don't often get a glimpse behind the façade people present, as they go about their day shopping, at a café, at the gym. How are they feeling really?

So don't feel bad you're not doing as well as others, and remember other people struggle too. Just because people do a great job of acting like they're fine, doesn't mean they are.

190 Go to a gig

It was very hot, very sweaty, very noisy.

We were crowded together in the dark in a small venue in Norwich.

Anticipating. Excited.

Those familiar moments when you're waiting for the headline band to appear.

Then there's a whoop from the front, silhouetted figures emerge on stage, the lights go up and BAM!

As Johnny Marr and his band opened with the first song of their set, 'The Tracers', we were transformed.

That incredible energy in a room full of strangers.

'We're ALIVE!!!' I shouted in my wife's ear as the music pulsed through us.

191 Take the slow route to the office

Nick Creswell – who we met in Idea #14 – is a friend of mine who lives in Camden, north London. In 2010 he got offered a new job. He was really excited about the role but was dreading the commute. It was based at Canary Wharf, out to the east of the city.

Thousands of people work in the Canary Wharf towers and the adjacent tube station gets really busy. It was a demanding role and Nick wanted to arrive in the right frame of mind.

But then he realized: he could take the boat to work! He could take the slow route from the London Eye down the river to Canary Wharf.

Nick did that from day one. Most mornings the riverboat was not even half full. Nick could get a seat and collect his thoughts or stand at the back of the boat and look at the sights as it travelled under Tower Bridge. It's a less efficient way of commuting, involving an earlier start, but he always arrived more energized than if he'd taken the tube. Nick reckons it's the best commute in London. And I agree!

192 Improve your commute

Exercise

Do you travel by train, tube or bus to work? How can you improve how you spend your commute?

Here are some ideas to get you started:

1. Close your eyes and scan your body for how you're feeling. Listen to a meditation app to help.
2. Put your phone away and notice what you can see out of the window.
3. Get off one stop early and walk the rest of the way.
4. Start your Good Times list.

5. Visualize – really picture – the rest of the day going well. Success at a meeting, a positive interaction with a client and so on.

6. Get your notepad out and get scribbling ideas for a side project.

193 Know how to deal with curve balls

Just when you think you have everything under control, an unexpected challenge gets thrown your way.

I asked my friend Sarah King, a seasoned entrepreneur, her advice for dealing with curve balls.

First, recognize they are inevitable. They don't happen because you have done something wrong.

Two, when a curve ball lands in your lap, hit pause. Don't act straight away.

Third, develop future sight. Can you pre-empt other issues that might occur in the future? If so, how would you respond to them?

Fourth, learn to enjoy them. Sarah likens it to being on Centre Court at Wimbledon up against Serena Williams in a fast rally. It's exhausting and you're calling on every last reserve of energy, but you're an active player in the game. Whether you win with a passing shot or you lose the point you will have learnt something, as well as knowing you've given your all. And that will set you up better for the next curve ball!

194 Open the empathy valve

On the birth of his second child Kevin Maguire struggled to cope. He couldn't connect with his son. He didn't know what was wrong. It was only on reading an article by a doctor who'd had a similar experience that Kevin realized he was suffering from paternal postnatal depression.

Kevin decided to write about his experience and share his story. He's since launched an email newsletter, 'The New Fatherhood' with the mission to change the narrative around male mental health and help men become comfortable sharing their emotions.

On a call from his home in Barcelona, Kevin told me that being open and vulnerable has released the empathy valve – it's given him a superpower to connect with how others are feeling. He's sending out a signal that says 'it's OK to feel like this' and is enabling a frank discussion about emotions. Men now regularly reach out to Kevin and say his story has helped them through a difficult time. Kevin believes we can have more meaningful conversations with others, and become better husbands, fathers and friends, when we're open and honest.

195 Reconnect with 'eros'

Psychologist Esther Perel's parents were the sole Holocaust survivors of their respective families. On an ABC Radio podcast Esther described what she noticed while growing up in Belgium. Many Holocaust survivors were understandably overcome with sorrow. Some however, Esther said, looked to maintain a sense of aliveness. They realized they had survived. They'd got a second chance and were going to make the best of life.

These survivors had a zest for conversation, music, dancing, gathering people together and savouring the beauty of life. Even after the horrors they'd experienced, they wanted to feel enjoyment again. Esther says they had imbued the concept of 'eros' – as an antidote to death, eros embraces a sense of curiosity, aliveness and exploration. It's what kept them going.

That sense of eros got passed on to Esther, who was speaking about this in the context of the world getting back to usual after the pandemic. How people are desperate for surprise and spontaneity. How a disaster heightens our sense of mortality, of that feeling 'life is short'.

Embracing eros can keep you alive, even in the most harrowing of situations.

196 Continue those family rituals

We're dancing around the kitchen playing saucepan drums with wooden spoons.

Or we're driving through country roads on holiday, perhaps we're feeling grumpy, and then we put our car song, 'Can You Dig It?' by The Mock Turtles on full blast. Then everything is okay again.

I am sure you have your family rituals. Sometimes it's just about lighting the candles at dinner or gathering around the record player for Sunday Record Club.

They're small things, but a signal. Something to turn to on a difficult day or when you just need to unite again, find some commonality, have a shared experience, just for the sake of it.

197 If you want to move others, first move yourself

David Hieatt – who we met in Idea #108 – is co-founder of the Do Lectures and Hiut Denim. A gifted storyteller, David stays hands-on when it comes to creating content for online courses, newsletters and other communications.

I wanted to know – how does he continuously and eloquently persuade people to act: to read, buy, sign up to stuff?

On a call from his farm in Wales, David told me he sees the writing process as a transference of energy. If you want to move other people, he says, first you have to move yourself. That's why David starts his day with a sea swim, or yoga or doing Wim Hof breathing techniques. It means that when he flips up his laptop lid, David's in the best space possible to transfer that energy through his writing.

Want to create work that motivates your audience to act? Get in an energetic mindset.

198 Record a Laughie

We all know what a selfie is, but have you heard of a Laughie?

Invented by health researcher Freda Gonot-Schoupinsky, a Laughie is when you record 60 seconds of your own laughter on your phone, either audio or with video.

You then play it back and laugh with it for the duration of one minute. Freda says that the benefits of laughter – decreasing stress hormones, boosting our immune system, reducing pain and increasing mood – are similar to those you get from exercise. The Laughie was designed as a laughter prescription, to ensure we all get at least one minute a day of laughter. Research of 25 to 93-year-olds found that using the Laughie, one minute three times a day over seven days, improved wellbeing.

199 Get social snacking

There's a lot in this book about the joy of talking to strangers. I'm a big fan of those random encounters, although I realize it can feel uncomfortable starting a conversation with someone you don't know.

So I asked my go-to expert Dr Hazel Harrison – who we met in Idea #90 – about it.

She told me that when you think about talking to a stranger, you tend to overestimate the awkwardness and under-estimate the benefit.

That explains a lot about our reticence at times to give it a go. So if you need a bit more convincing, Hazel says that interacting with strangers gives you a sense of belonging. You may put your best self forward, so it puts you in a good space. And you'll probably get a dopamine hit too, the chemical that plays a part in how you feel pleasure.

And if you talk to a stranger and it goes well, it reinforces further engagement. Hazel sees it as a form of social-snacking, a bite-sized way of keeping your human connections going.

200 Look for the spark of connection

When a stranger from Boulder, Colorado commented on a photo I shared on Twitter, I responded. Cali and I then began an online conversation. Cali – who's starting up a new venture, North Star Rising – felt like a kindred spirit, so we lined up a Zoom. And now every month or so, we have a call and talk about what we're up to in our work life.

When I spoke to her last week it was first thing in the morning Mountain Time. I asked her what she needs to have a good day, and she said – a spark of connection.

Cali said it could be an exchange with the barista that goes beyond a 'Hi'. Or a belly laugh with one of her nephews over a silly joke. Or perhaps a deep, connected conversation with someone.

For her, it's that little glimmer that sparkles to life, when two people really see each other for who they are. It's an apt response from someone I immediately felt a connection with.

201 Alert your mind by going somewhere new

I like to work in a nomadic way. When I'm travelling to another city, I might rack up 15 to 20 different spaces – from coffee shops to hotel lobbies – that

I work from in a single week. I always love those experiences. I have clear memories of these trips. Right now I'm recalling a sunny morning in a café in Madrid. I was only there for an hour but I can remember so much.

The *Financial Times* columnist Tim Harford has written about the power of going somewhere new and how a week full of new experiences will seem longer compared to the same week back home. Visiting different cities – hotels, restaurants, cafés, plane cabins, train carriages – in the same week, time goes a lot slower than if you had the same Monday-to-Friday routine.

And that's because Tim says that our brains record a new physical place with particular vividness. Your mind is more alert.

202 Choose the right tools

A smooth-writing pen. A special notepad.

Whether journalling, writing a birthday card to a friend or scribbling some work notes in a coffee shop, the right tools matter. I can't just use any pen, especially if what I'm working on is important. My pen of choice is a Muji 0.5 nib or my special Kawaeco Sport that my wife bought me. As for pencils, blunt ones don't cut it.

There's something about decent stationery. It just makes writing a pleasure. PaperSmiths in Clifton, Bristol; Choosing Keeping in London; CW Pencils on New York's Lower East Side: whenever I'm in these cities I make a beeline for these treasure troves.

203 Look at things from a different perspective

When I reached out to my work friend Helen Tupper for advice, we set a date to meet at an art gallery.

Tate Modern proved a dramatic – and effective – backdrop for our chat. We started at the top and worked our way down. At the bottom, we wandered into an installation by Olafur Eliasson called 'Room for One Colour'.

The area was illuminated by mono-frequency lamps that suppressed all colours except yellow and black. All we could see in front of us were shades of grey. It was disorientating, like a filter had been placed over the room and everyone in it. We both agreed we'd never had such a strange experience like it.

Eliasson says he designed the installation to demonstrate that our perception is not fixed but changes with our environment. With his play with light, he is seeking to replicate our experience of seeing the world from multiple perspectives.

How apt that was, being with Helen – and Olafur – who helped me see my work life from an alternative perspective on that wonderful afternoon. Sometimes you just need a different way of looking at things to get the right answer.

204 Make the most of your lunch hour

It's too easy to start work at 9am and to work through to 6pm five days a week, consumed with the tasks in hand and rarely coming up for air. How you spend your days becomes how you spend your life, and I don't want to lose my life to pure grind.

Many people don't even leave their desk – let alone their office – to eat lunch, even though taking a proper lunch break, especially when it's not only to eat, can provide unexpected benefits.

One lunchtime when I was working from home, the band Mystery Jets happened to be playing a set at a local record shop. It was two train stops away, so too good to miss. It made a great punctuation mark to the day and it felt like a treat. It was such an intimate gig. They were great.

There will always be days when you get thrown curve balls and you don't have time to get out at lunch. But when you can, whether it's going for a walk, browsing the bookstore or heading to a lunchtime set by one of your favourite bands – feed yourself.

205 Improve your lunch hour

Exercise

Do you have a lunch hour at work? How do you spend it – do you go to the gym, sit with a sandwich at your desk, or go out for a walk?

What are the steps you could take to improve your lunch hour, what could you do to make it better?

Here are some simple ideas to get you started:

1. Go for a walk in an alternative direction to one you usually take and be curious – look around, what do you spot?

2. Visit somewhere specific – is there a park, museum or other space nearby you can wander around?

3. Buy a magazine you wouldn't normally read and take it, along with your lunch, and sit on a park bench.

4. Go for a run or a swim.

What else could you do?

206 Celebrate blossom season

Walking the dog on an unremarkable suburban street yesterday, I passed a tree that was in full blossom. It was beautiful. I stopped to take it in, aware that the blossom will be soon gone.

Far from the suburban streets of my native Essex, Japan is famous for its fleeting cherry blossom – *sakura* – season. The blossoms last only for a few days. The Japanese celebrate its appearance with family get-togethers and parties – *hanami* – under the trees. The celebration is about appreciating the transience of life, the fleeting nature of things.

Understanding that such things are short-lived and transient helps you accept the ebb and flow of life, to appreciate what you have as it's happening and, when it passes, to accept it's gone.

207 Let up on yourself

I'm fortunate that I have a lot of flexibility in my working life, yet still my default setting used to be to squeeze so much out of every moment of the day. Travelling around the country by train, I used to set a task or exercise for each part of the journey. A podcast to listen to for this section. A document to edit for this one. Research notes to review in a café.

After a while it became overwhelming. So I changed things. On the outbound journey I still filled my day with things that needed to be done, but on the return journey I'd let up on myself.

Heading back from Newcastle or Cardiff I'd order a gin and tonic from the trolley. Watch a documentary. Read a novel. There was no pressure.

Life got better when I stopped trying to be too efficient with my time and I allowed space to just be.

208 Swap the tube for a walk

One Monday morning I was headed to a meeting at Victoria. The tube was crowded, I didn't have a seat and all I could focus on was hanging on to the strap above my head and to avoid bumping into the person next to me.

I was one stop away from my destination, but I'd had enough of being a sardine, so I thought I'd try something: walk the rest of the way. When the doors next opened, I hopped off.

Overground, my two feet took me crunching through the autumn leaves of St James's Park. What a contrast to the stifling tube carriage. It was exactly what I needed.

Sarah Ellis, co-author of *The Squiggly Career* and host of the podcast of the same name, told me she likes to do the same on her London days. Walking instead of tubing it gets her brain as well as her body moving.

Sarah says it gets her unstuck, prompts new ideas and provides a boost of energy and optimism. She acknowledges that a walk can feel like a luxury when your to-do list is overwhelming but, for her, walking = better working.

209 Pay your respects

Adam was a lovely guy who I knew from my local coffee shop where we were both regulars. When I think of him now I can picture his big smile, standing at the counter talking to Simon about last night's football.

Adam was diagnosed with cancer. It was terrible to hear of his death a year or so later. He was a young man with a lovely warm spirit.

I knew the date of Adam's funeral but felt awkward about going. I wasn't a friend or family and didn't want to intrude. I was a distant acquaintance, simply knowing him because we both liked coffee.

But then you only get one chance to pay your respects. His presence had touched me, now was the time to honour his life. It was testament to what a special person he was that the chapel was so full of people who felt the same way that it was standing room only.

210 Follow the good coffee

While I love coffee, I really love *good* coffee. And my search for a quality Long Black often takes me off the beaten track.

I'm always happy to make an effort to seek it out.

In Madrid I walked a couple of miles to find Federal Café.

In Belfast I hurried through the rain to get to Established Coffee.

In Berlin, I took a detour down Sophienstraße and stumbled upon a little coffee shop where I talked to the owner Ben. He told me he'd always dreamed of opening his own place.

Finding those places and having those conversations feels like a fast-track to get to know the city. To feel like a local.

I remember one morning in Liverpool where I'd searched out 92 Degrees coffee shop.

When I sat down it wasn't only the coffee I enjoyed. The ideas flowed and my productivity and creativity were boosted. My senses were awakened. I got things done. I'm always glad I hunt out the good coffee.

CHAPTER 8
TURN LEFT

211 Remember – this is life itself

If you have, or had, young children you'll likely know it can be stressful trying to get them ready for school. Trying to leave the house, not only so they're on time, but to ensure you can catch your train or make your appointment.

You'll also know that 'they grow up so fast!' might be a cliché, but it's true.

It struck me one day that walking my two sons to primary school was a highlight of my life. I focused on savouring it before it became too late.

Like the author Gretchen Rubin reflected on her bus rides to school with her daughter – the days are long, but the years are short. It's that recognition that this is parenthood, this is the childhood of her daughter, this is life itself.

I'm glad I had that realization. I wrote this in my notebook of April 2015:

> 'I know that one day they won't want to hold my hand.
> One day they will walk to school by themselves. And one day
> I will miss walking them to school like crazy.'

212 Be a Julia!

It was a lovely sunny morning and I stopped by Monmouth Coffee in London's Covent Garden. I grabbed my coffee in a paper cup and headed outside.

There were two men sitting outside on the bench, one with a pushchair. I asked if there was space for one more and they parted so I could sit in the middle.

Holding my full coffee cup in my right hand, I took the left backpack strap off my shoulder and then let it slip down. As it did, it juddered down the length of my arm, violently shaking my hand. I had thrown hot coffee over myself, showering my jeans. Damn!

And then I looked to my left. I'd thrown hot coffee over the man with the pushchair.

And he was wearing white jeans.

WTF! I ran inside to get help. When something awkward happens, there's usually someone who will save the day and make things better. And that day it was Julia. She came out with paper towels. She offered somewhere for the guy to clean up. She even said, poor you – let me get you another coffee.

How much the Julias of the world make embarrassing situations a tiny bit better! Thank you Julia.

213 Hard-bake self-care into your working day

Sarah King – who we met in Idea #193 – is co-founder of 'we are radikl', a movement and network that helps female entrepreneurs make their business ideas happen. It can be pressured building your own business, and Sarah makes sure self-care is factored into her working practices. It's not just about taking time off.

Being clear on her priorities means she can be present in what she's doing. And at the same time she consciously de-prioritizes what won't get done in order to create the space she needs. Doing this gives her a sense of focus and calm – she's embedded this practice to benefit not only herself but those around her.

She confesses she doesn't get it right all the time, and that's OK – as Sarah acknowledges, part of self-care is being kind to yourself. And by its very nature, a practice means noticing, learning, improving – it's not about getting it perfect from the off.

214 Go for a run in the rain

It was pouring with rain so I really didn't fancy going for a run.

But I'd put it in my calendar for 4pm, so when my phone pinged me a reminder I felt like I'd made a commitment.

No excuses, just go.

The first ten minutes were miserable. I ran up the hill, cursing the wind and rain as I went. But at the top, the rain stopped, and the light peeked through the clouds. Then suddenly the sun broke through, illuminating the blossom on the trees and glinting off the newly wet streets.

What struck me then, in that moment where we were all bathed in that wonderful afternoon light, was this: if you don't go for a run in the rain, you won't see the sun come out.

215 Be a monk for the morning!

It can be hard to focus if you're always checking social media or your inbox is clamouring for your attention.

So if you want to have breakthrough ideas, you need space for that.

And similarly, if what's on your to-do list is really important, you need to create the optimum working conditions.

The challenge for many of us is being able to do what author Cal Newport calls 'deep work'. Especially when interruptions and distractions constantly pester you for your time.

To do the work that really matters, Newport suggests a 'Monk Mode Morning' where no meetings, alerts or pings of any kind are allowed.

If a whole morning is unrealistic, carve out a more manageable Monk Mode Hour every day where you put up a 'do not disturb sign' by silencing your phone, closing down your email. Then get immersed in the most important tasks of the day.

216 Ask people what they think

A few years ago I was hired to run an important annual meeting for an organization. The company wanted to revitalize the meeting by getting an outsider in. I didn't know anything about their industry so all I could do was to facilitate the discussion in my own way.

Whenever an important issue was raised, I went round the room asking everyone present a simple question.

'What do you think?'

The next week I telephoned my client for feedback. She said it had gone well.

I asked why.

Because, she said, you asked what we thought. A small question has a big impact, and gets to the heart of the matter.

217 Let Georgia boost your day

Through the wonders of Twitter and the fact that I follow US radio station 90.3 KEXP-FM Seattle, I had a lovely moment on Monday when I clicked on a video they had shared.

It was a performance by London-based producer, songwriter, singer, rapper and drummer Georgia.

The video is of her in a studio, jumping around playing drums and a keyboard, and belting out a cover of the Kate Bush classic 'Running Up That Hill'. It connected with me. It was impossible to ignore Georgia's energy.

The tweet from KEXP said, 'Skyrocket into your week' and they were right.

218 Open the door for the UPS man

A Monday morning. I wasn't feeling in a great mood as I headed out of the train station and walked towards my 9 o'clock meeting. As I strolled up the street I passed a UPS delivery guy in his brown uniform, reversing a trolley piled high with parcels and heading into an office building.

It wasn't an automatic door. I could see he was going to struggle.

So I manoeuvred myself ahead and opened the door for him.

That was it.

We exchanged a smile. That simple interaction really lifted me. I hadn't just held open a door for him, he'd opened a door into a brighter Monday morning.

I had a spring in my step after that.

219 Have a snack of creativity

Did you know that when you are engaged in creative activities, you're in a relaxed state, so it sends a signal to the brain that you feel safe?

You can use that to your advantage. If you want to get a safe, relaxed mindset – get creative! Even quick bursts of such activity are beneficial. Clinical psychologist Dr Hazel Harrison calls these 'creative snacks' that get those neurochemicals flowing.

I love that. So alongside your mid-morning coffee, forgo the biscuit and have a creative snack instead! There's something liberating when you're just playing, when you don't care about the output. For Hazel, it might be a doodle, colouring, moving art around the wall.

You don't need to share it or show it. Just snack on it.

220 Arrive on a high

Once a week Giles Pearman cycles from his home in Teddington to his client's office at Oxford Circus in central London. It's 15 miles each way. The journey takes him through the majestic expanse of Richmond Park, along the Thames in Putney and then through Hyde Park to Marble Arch.

He told me how yesterday's ride had been perfect. He doesn't rush the journey but savours it. As he cycled along the Thames by Putney he passed the boat club where rowers were getting into the water. The scene was spectacular, like something on a film set.

So when he arrived at the office, having grabbed his takeout coffee, he was on a high. A recognition that this was a really good day. And he'd only just got started.

221 Look after your guests like Nikos

We were on holiday with our three-year-old and one-year-old boys at a small hotel in Crete.

On the first night our three-year-old woke up in pain. It was 2am in a foreign country. We had no hire car and no idea about doctors or hospitals. It was a tiny hotel which wasn't staffed overnight. We dialled the emergency number that had been provided. It turned out to be the mobile phone of the owner, Nikos, who lived a short drive away.

Fortunately Nikos picked up the phone. When he discovered he couldn't get a doctor out to us, he drove over to collect my wife and son and took them to hospital. There, he acted as translator as they saw a doctor. Nikos then drove my wife to a pharmacy to get the medicine – which he insisted on paying for. He then returned them to the hotel.

In the morning I went to thank him so much for all he had done and to apologize for his interrupted night.

He just replied, 'It was nothing'.

222 Connect over a shared story

The very essence of what makes us human is our interaction with others. A shared connection with another human being, however fleeting, makes the world go round.

Aimee lives in the Pacific Northwest. She works as a storyteller for one of the world's biggest companies. These moments of connectedness are essential for Aimee to have a good day, when she has the strong yet often ephemeral feeling she's on the same page as someone else, and a part of a broader community.

She told me it can be around the small things: a song, a memory, a person or place in common, a shared story. It gives her the realization she's not alone but knitted into the broader fabric of the universe. When they occur, the interactions fuel her, giving Aimee her best days.

223 Pop your head around the corner

My phone pinged. A WhatsApp from my old friend Pascal, who I'd not heard from for months: 'just popping my head around the corner, seeing how you're doing?'

That made me smile. I like that image of a mate sticking his head round, checking in on me. Who can you send a WhatsApp message to right now simply to say you are thinking of someone or to see how they're doing?

Twenty seconds' thumb action might just make someone's day.

224 Be intentional about your habits

I was talking to my new friend Cali – who we met in Idea #200 – about our respective coffee routines. How having a decent coffee is an important part of the day.

I said that most mornings I grab a takeout. Or I'll make a pot for me and my wife. If it's just me, I'll use the Aeropress.

Cali said she liked making coffee the Aeropress way too. She says it feels very intentional.

I hadn't thought about that. Taking the Aeropress kit out, placing a filter paper in the device. Spooning in coffee, adding water. Stirring. Plunging. There's a process that adds something to the making and the enjoying.

It's more deliberate, more thought-through and yes, more intentional. For me, it amplifies something that might otherwise be mundane and heightens its significance.

225 Head up to the walkways

It was 11:45am, and the elevated walkways in the City of London were quiet. There was hardly anyone about.

As soon as I climbed the steps and headed west on these newly renovated paths, I felt my head buzzing with ideas and clarity. Up above the traffic, walking between office buildings on the curving, winding path got me in a really good frame of mind. Up here I seemed to slow down and be able to find clarity on issues I'd been wrestling with.

By the time I'd arrived down at street level I felt I'd turbo-charged my Wednesday morning. I looked at my watch and realized I'd only been up on the walkway for eight minutes!

Finding another space that allows an opportunity to think might just be what's needed to get the creative juices flowing. Get up and go somewhere different and see what it does for you.

226 Get in flow on the dance floor

Dancing is a joyous activity with a host of other benefits, such as the power to fuel your creative thinking.

There is a well-established link between movement and creative thinking: when you move, it gets the ideas flowing. Peter Lovatt – who we met in Idea #36 – explains that dance takes it one step further, with different types of movement influencing different types of thinking and problem solving. Dancing, he says, is a full-brain workout – the more you move in a variety of ways the more you'll stimulate diverse thoughts.

So get waving those hands in the air (like you just don't care), and get a fresh perspective on what's on your mind.

227 Pick up a magazine

I have a confession to make – I have a magazine habit.

I'm drawn to bookshops and newsstands. I love to walk away with a magazine.

Do You Read Me in Berlin. Magma in London. The Athenaeum Nieuwscentrum in Amsterdam. These are some of my favourite places for browsing magazines, picking up familiar titles like *The New Yorker*, *Monocle* and *Courier*, but also discovering ones I've never heard of.

When I pick up *Monocle*, it provides me a window onto those streets and urban scenes I love so much. Tokyo. Copenhagen. São Paulo. Giving me a taste of what's out there – it always fuels me.

For the price of a couple of coffees or a bottle of wine, you can be inspired, surprised and delighted.

228 Rekindle those old friendships

Do you have an old friendship that's important to you, but you've neglected?

It's never too late to reach out to someone again. Especially if you and the friend go way back together.

My go-to expert on friendships, Dr Hazel Harrison, says that relationships made during our adult life need nurturing or they'll fizzle out. But she added that friendships we form in childhood or at college don't require the same level of maintenance and are easier to rekindle when they've been dormant.

Last year I reached out to my old friend Claire, who I met at college in 1987. We'd barely been in touch the last 15 years or so. We had a lovely catch-up on FaceTime. Even though we hadn't seen each other for so long, we made each other laugh and had plenty to chat about.

It's a lovely feeling when you slip back into the old way of being together. With Claire it took me right back to those lecture halls and our shared student house in Headingley.

229 Hold an awards ceremony at work

When I quit my role as managing director of a radio studio company, I like to think I left a legacy. After all, I'd made the business more commercially successful and had recruited a great team.

One of the things I really love being remembered for was not a financial achievement or anything strategic to the growth of the company. It was that every year I hosted an awards ceremony.

We'd make a big night of it. I'd write a jokey script. There'd be champagne. A PA system. A music bed for each category. Nominations. We had plastic Oscar figurines to give out.

And on the night, we had such a great time. I loved it.

And you know what, if that's what people remember from my time there, I'm happy with that.

230 Shine a light on your local community

John Waire – who we met in Idea #8 – is a photographer who's based in Baltimore. He's a generous guy who is always looking for the positive in life. And it's a pleasure to know him.

He always signs his emails with the words, 'shine your light'.

John cares about his community and wants to make sure his city pushes out the negativity and highlights all the good that's happening.

He cared so much, he started a movement. He called it 'Shine Your Light Baltimore'. He got t-shirts printed. And then he had a crazy idea about getting a huge 'Shine Your Light' mural painted on a wall. So he launched a crowdfunding campaign to make it happen. It was a lovely moment to see him share a photograph of the finished mural.

John told me he wants to ensure people are aware of all of the good they are surrounded by. To spread that positive energy around.

I bet many more of us could benefit from a 'Shine Your Light' movement in our cities and neighbourhoods.

231 Pat an explorer on the back

In 2020, Quintin Lake completed his five-year, 10,000-km walk around the coast of Britain. In those last few weeks I followed his progress on

Twitter as he made his slow way around the tributaries of the Essex coast.

His feat was impressive as he travelled alone, pitching a tent at the end of each day, waking up the next morning drawing on all his reserves of energy and commitment to keep going.

Soon he would come through my home town, in fact, he'd be passing along the coastal path at the bottom of my road. When you think of all the effort Quintin was making it felt lazy of me not to go and greet him!

So I went out with my friend Dave to welcome him. 'Welcome to Leigh-on-Sea!' we called out as he reached us. We bought him a coffee and walked two kilometres with him before wishing him well as he headed towards the finish line of London.

I would have hated to think of him walking through my town without any recognition for his achievement – I am glad Dave and I appointed ourselves the unofficial welcoming party.

232 Don't wait 49 years before you get a dog

I'd wanted a dog all my life.

And 2002 was probably the perfect year to get one. Newly single and newly self-employed, I suddenly had a lot of flexibility in my life. And to be honest, I was feeling lonely.

It would have been the perfect time to drive the short distance to Battersea Dogs Home and ask about a dog.

But I didn't. Perhaps I made up some reasons to convince myself why it wasn't a good idea.

Sukie – a border terrier – finally arrived in my life when I was 49.

Unsurprisingly, she has improved my quality of life.

So my advice is don't wait nearly five decades to get or do that thing. Take a chance.

Okay we're not all dog lovers, so it doesn't have to be a four-legged friend.

Whatever you've wanted for years, whatever is sacred to you, do it now.

233 Turn left

A Thursday morning a few years ago. Walking down the road, I saw an old school friend.

As we got to the railway station at the bottom of the road, he turned right towards the ticket barriers to head up to his job in the City of London.

And I turned left.

I walked over the footbridge to the seafront. I looked out to the big skies of the Thames estuary, felt for my notebook and pen in my pocket and hit 'play' on my podcast.

I saw my friend again the following week. This time it was on the platform, I was getting an early train to host a breakfast event. He beckoned me over to join him. 'They're a bit bright!' he said, looking down at my red Adidas trainers.

Sometimes 'turning left' is about taking a different path in your career. Other times it's making sure you stick to your personality, wearing red shoes.

Turning left is how I make choices in life. Taking the path marked Me. Not following the crowd.

Doing things my way. Choosing to be different.

234 Listen to your eight-year-old self

Can you remember what you were like when you were eight?

I can.

I loved drawing. I liked playing with my Matchbox cars and with Lego. I liked reading books. I was curious, I loved finding facts in *The Guinness Book of Records*. I got a school prize for reading. I was a quiet kid, with a strong sense of who I was and what I liked.

Nearly 40 years later, I found myself on stage at the Do Lectures. I told a story I'd not shared before, of how in my 20s I got lost in life. How I went through a difficult time that resulted in me quitting my job. I told the audience that when I got lost I should have asked my eight-year-old self for directions. I strongly feel he would have known which way to go.

As I clicked the button during my Do Lecture, a photograph of the eight-year-old Ian appeared on the screen behind me. Standing on a seawall, a satchel around his neck, looking through binoculars.

He had the answer.

235 Make time for the *sobremesas*

You know that feeling when you've had a really good meal in a restaurant or have hosted a dinner at home. You're with friends or family. You've eaten well, the plates have been cleared away and now it's time for a jug of coffee or a tot of Limoncello.

And now the really important postprandial conversations can happen.

The Spanish have a word for it: the *sobremesas*. That ritual of staying at the table after a meal and putting the world to rights. Voices may get raised. People will talk politics or football. Or swap some gossip. There'll probably be a lot of laughter too.

I love that. That sense of savouring the experience and not rushing off.

236 Get yourself a birthday present

We think nothing of choosing a birthday present for a family member or best friend, but it might sound self-indulgent that we do the same for ourselves.

I believe it's important that we invest time and attention on what we need to thrive. We care about our loved ones, let's care about ourselves too.

When it was my 50th birthday I treated myself to an easyJet flight and a concert ticket to see Johnny Marr play at the Amsterdam venue, Melkweg.

There's something about seeing Johnny live that I find magnetic. That talent, that 'no f***s given' spirit. I go away creatively charged, confident to be me.

Standing there in Melkweg as 'Bigmouth Strikes Again' started up – a track I'd grown up with 35 years earlier – it sent a tingle up my spine. The teenage Ian would be proud to know that for his 50th birthday gift, I'd go and see Johnny Marr at a venue I'd first visited during my InterRail trip back in 1986.

237 Make your colleagues feel loved

One Valentine's Day in a previous role, Claire Van der Zant bought cards for everyone in her team at work. She personalized each card, writing a message to every colleague saying how grateful she was for their contribution. She left the cards on their desks to be discovered when they arrived in the morning. The impact it had was enormous – everyone loved her cards. One recipient said it had been one of the most important gestures an employer had shown in her entire career. For another, it trumped the less-than-impressive card she'd received from her husband that morning (oh dear).

It made a lasting impression long after the roses had wilted.

238 Sleep for seven hours

Matthew Walker, author of *Why We Sleep*, is keen for us to get more of this nightly necessity – at least seven hours a night. Fewer than seven hours and he claims you're damaging yourself as much as drinking or smoking to excess. Sleep is necessary for good health. Benefits include helping keep your weight in check, extending longevity and batting away colds and flu.

As for caffeine, it stays in your body longer than you might think. If you drink coffee at midday, then 12 hours later your brain still has 25 per cent of the caffeine. It doesn't leave your system until between 24 and 36 hours later (woah – who knew!).

Some of us unfortunately don't have good nights' sleep for whatever reason, despite trying every solution in the book. If that's you, I feel for you.

And if you're having those early afternoon flat whites, you might want to switch to decaff.

239 Make friends with your neighbours

For 14 years I lived in a small house at the end of a little mews in southwest London. A mews is narrower than a street and the houses have no back gardens so life tends to happen on the cobbles out front, among the parked cars and tubs of plants. There were 12 properties in my mews. Some were newly renovated, others had workshops or garages below and accommodation above. Elderly people who had been there for decades lived alongside young newcomers. My next door neighbour was a photographer, and on the other side of him lived a milkman.

There were so many wonderful stories in that mews, but for the first seven years of living there, we didn't chat that much beyond a hello or a wave. Then Georg and Yvonne moved in opposite. They'd moved over from Germany and in a few months had made their impact on this small community. They organized an annual mews summer party. We put a line of tables out in the middle, fired up the BBQ and gathered around. It was wonderful.

Danke schön to my lovely German friends for getting us all together and enhancing our lives.

240 Stumble upon the special

My hotel in Glasgow was not in a glamorous location. It was down by the river and to get anywhere you had to walk underneath the busy A814 highway. But once I was out the other side I found Finnieston, a buzzy neighbourhood of cafés and shops. And then one afternoon out exploring I walked past a restaurant called Ox & Finch.

It seemed to signal me, so I stopped, walked back and booked for later that evening. A few hours later, I was sitting up at a table.

Sitting there I felt: this was my place. It was one of the best meals of my life. No question. So much so, I returned the next night.

That sense of random discovery is really rewarding. The best experiences are stumbled upon, not planned.

CHAPTER 9

PUT YOUR HAND UP IF YOU NEED A HARD HAT

241 Be your own historian

There's a photo of me at 18. I'm standing at the back of an open van, boxes of vinyl spread out in front of me. A summer job selling records at a music festival.

It's funny how photographs of you growing up can define you all these years later.

They are the pictures that enable you to tell your story, good and bad. They are in your memory bank.

When you become the historian of your own life, you can take meaning from your story, connecting the dots between the milestones and memories.

As my friend Jerry Colonna (who we first met in Idea #96) told me, opening up the box of your past and flipping through the photographs of your past self is more than just pure nostalgia. It is, he says, about examining the question of who you are.

Do you have an old box of photos? Take time to hit the rewind button and recall those stories, memories and experiences that have shaped you.

What do you take from those photos about who you are today?

242 Give your soul some soil

A ten-foot-high sunflower springs from a street corner in urban Brooklyn. This is the site of Keap Fourth – at the intersection of Brooklyn's Keap and South 4th streets – just one of hundreds of community gardens that have sprouted from the street corners of New York City.

Keap Fourth's (follow them on Instagram @keapfourthgarden) mission is to provide the local community access to green space and fresh healthy food. Volunteers and activists have turned abandoned lots into urban oases where local residents can go to relax or plant vegetables.

My friend Emily's garden in west Yorkshire is a long way from Brooklyn, but she shares that love of the soil. Getting her hands dirty, planting and tending.

In her garden in Yorkshire Emily feels more connected with her surroundings – that puts her in a good mood. What is it about the soil? According to Emily there's a theory that the smell of the earth brings feelings of wellbeing. It's because our primitive brain recognizes there's water present, and water equals survival and safety.

Whether you're doing it alone or in a group, getting your hands dirty helps boost your soul.

243 Cut to the chase

I love that scene in the film *Annie Hall* when Alvy asks Annie for a kiss. She's surprised at his directness – it's at the start of their first date – but he tells her it'll be better if they get it over with early. It will save all that tension later. If they kiss and get it done with, then they'll digest their food better.

I love the scene because I wish more of us had the courage to be that direct with each other.

'I fancy you, would you have dinner with me?'

'I would love to work with you.'

Cut to the chase, be direct, say what you mean. And move on to the next course.

244 Don't worry about FOMO

I'm not on the latest audio-only social network app.

I don't follow football.

I've never seen an episode of *Game of Thrones*.

Sure, I know these three things might be amazing, might make a difference to my life.

But I'm okay thanks. I'll take that risk. I don't have unlimited bandwidth. I have to pick where I put my attention, and accept I'll never be across all things all the time. Some things have to give.

245 Come in, hang out, lean on us

Founded upon his passion for boardsports, New Zealander Steve Dunstan started the iconic clothing brand Huffer back in 1997.

If you're in Auckland, head to the brand's Huffer House store. Here Steve aims to provide a space for people – not only its customers but the community at large – to hang out. There is a kitchen area where people can drop in to chat and grab a free coffee in exchange for making a donation to the Mental Health Foundation. Steve is passionate about paying attention to mental health – and he wants the Huffer House to be like your own house: warm, supportive and sociable. Come in, hang out, lean on us, he says.

What a beautiful spirit. Isn't it wonderful to know that there are people all over the world intent on helping others have a good day, in a way that's authentic to them? Even if you're nowhere near Auckland, keep your radar switched on to those businesses near you trying to do the same.

246 If they make you fly, buy those boots!

A late December afternoon in Amsterdam. I walked past a shop and was seduced by what I saw in the window: a pair of olive green boots.

I really liked them, but came up with reasons why I didn't need them.

Back at the hotel I phoned my wife.

'Go buy them!' she said.

They're just a pair of boots. But there was something about them. I thought I'd like to wear them on stage.

So I retraced my steps. But the streets and canals suddenly all looked the same.

It was nearly 5.30pm. I couldn't go back tomorrow as I was heading home. But then, I spotted the shop: 15a Prinsenstraat. The shop owner told me the pair in the window were the last ones.

Did they fit?!

Now, they're my favourites. They make me fly!

247 Keep it clean

Rain or shine, I often see them on our daily walks along the beach, wearing blue tabards, picking up bottles, cans, coffee cups and cigarette butts among other unsavoury items. These wonderful people are volunteers with Southend Beach Care which has a number of teams tidying up my local beach.

While I remove the odd bottle or piece of plastic, I'm not out for an hour or so at a time, scooping up the rubbish other folk leave behind. Their dedication to keeping our stretch of coast clean is impressive.

There's something about clearing up other people's thoughtless mess that's heroic. Thank you for your work caring for a space we can all continue to enjoy.

248 Travel by phone

I've got 5,298 photographs on my phone dating back to 2009.

317 are of my children.

208 of my wife.

145 of books.

118 of dogs.

6 more of coffee than there are of the beach.

Quite a few are taken from trains and planes too.

What's wonderful is that on a grey and dull Monday morning in a train carriage, when it's still dark outside and the windows are misted up, I can scroll through these images and be transported back to family barbecues, children's parties or Mediterranean beaches.

Take a journey via your phone to relive some of the best memories of your life.

249 Put your hand up if you need a hard hat

At the age of 30 I'd been appointed managing director of a media company. On the surface things were going well for me. I had a job I enjoyed and was living in a pretty London mews house.

One evening I returned home to find a group of engineers wearing hard hats outside my house. The property was adjacent to a railway station, and I was told the embankment was cracking under pressure and the station platform was sinking. Trees and plants were soon replaced by scaffolding and heavy equipment.

I was soon living on a building site which operated throughout the night, six nights a week. As I tried to sleep, workmen walked along scaffolding that was only inches from my bedroom wall. Cranes swung overhead. Drills vibrated, generators whirred. During the 18 months of works, I logged 130 interrupted or lost nights of sleep.

And at work I was cracking up too. I had too much on my plate and couldn't cope.

I'd needed my own hard hat. But I didn't put my hand up and ask for help until it was too late. When things get tough at work, flag it. Don't suffer in silence. Get the help you need.

250 Surprise yourself and pull it off

Giving talks, running workshops and facilitating discussions are now an established part of my business. When I started out however, I'd often commit to a new project and then think, oh wow, this is really out of my comfort zone. I've never done one quite like this before. How am I going to do it?

It got to be a theme. My wife would often tease me: 'what on earth have you got yourself into this time?!'

But I'd get ready for these gigs the only way I knew how: with a mountain of planning and preparation. And armed with my material and tools I'd go and deliver whatever it was I'd been hired to do.

And here's the thing – these gigs would go okay! I'd get into my stride and enjoy myself. Then I'd ring Zoë and joke, 'phew, I got away with it again!'

That sense of 'getting away with it' is not about winging it or being unprofessional. It's a sense of going out of your comfort zone, challenging yourself and working super hard so you can pull it off.

251 Rediscover your neighbourhood

When the BBC asked me to run a series of workshops around the UK getting teams to be more curious and creative, I knew what I needed to do: get them outside!

So I sent my participants out onto the streets for an hour in order to notice the world about them. It's such a simple exercise, but one that yields great results.

An attendee in Glasgow told me she'd learned more about a neighbourhood in 45 minutes than she had in 20 years driving through the area to work. She'd stumbled across a café where she overheard conversations that had given her an unparalleled insight into the local community.

Getting unshackled from your desk is a way to notice, question and be present in your work environs, allowing more opportunities for those kinds of encounters that make for a good day.

252 Feel that sense of *Fernweh*

In my notebook I have a picture of the clear blue sea at Hermoupolis on the island of Syros.

Another of stunning gardens in Provence.

And one of Villa Arrighi, in the Niccone Valley in Umbria.

I haven't been to any of these places. These are photographs I've ripped out of magazines.

Whether I make it to these places or not remains to be seen, yet there's something seductive about these images and how they make me feel.

The Germans have a word for it: *Fernweh*. It's translated as a longing for distant places we have never been to.

A longing to travel to get away. A sense of hope. An imagining of sunnier climes. A sense of *Fernweh* can fill us with optimism about a trip we hope to make. Or simply fill us with pleasure in the knowledge that these places exist somewhere out there in the world. On dull or wintery days, losing yourself in such images can bring the sunshine right in.

253 Play team sports

Research shows that people who exercise – and particularly those who do so together in a team – demonstrate good mental health.

In an interview with *The Lancet Psychiatry*, Yale University's Adam Chekroud cites research that shows people who exercise had, on average, one and a half fewer days per month of poor mental health, than those who didn't exercise.

Individuals who played team sports like basketball and football posted the biggest reduction.

The key ways physical exercise can help your mental health, Chekroud says, are motivation to get moving, physical exertion, the social element and that feeling of mindfulness.

254 Listen up!

Kate Murphy is a *New York Times* journalist. A couple of years ago I was in the audience at a breakfast event about her book *You're Not Listening*. Kate told the story of observing a high-performing furniture salesman at work in a showroom. A couple were seated opposite having just taken an interest in some furniture. At the end of the conversation the salesman didn't fill the silence.

He sat there for what Kate felt was an uncomfortably long time.

He said nothing.

And then the couple announced they were going to buy everything!

Kate is someone who knows the importance of listening, and her book relates the stories of countless conversations she's had with everyone from priests to CIA interrogators to bartenders.

Whether we're a child, a partner, a team member, a friend, or a customer, sometimes we just want to be listened to, for our story to be heard, to not be talked over and not be second-guessed what we're going to say, do, or buy next.

When was the last time you really listened to someone, or someone really listened to you?

255 Don't beat yourself up

Like me, the entrepreneur David Hieatt is really interested in hacking the right habits and behaviours in order to have a good day. Part of that is managing his relationship with his phone. David aims to not look at his phone for the first hour of the day and then to put it away in the evening.

Most of the time.

David said there are occasions when he'll break his rule. And he's okay with that, because it aligns with his philosophy: that the default is the default, but exceptions are exceptions.

What he means is that being careful with his phone time remains his default position. It's what he'll always go back to. And when there are exceptions, he won't beat himself up.

If you manage to keep up a habit for 300 days a year, David says, but fall off the wagon for the rest, then he reckons that's a pretty good success rate. It's a forgiving position, as well as pragmatic, and much better than beating yourself up every time you let slip.

256 Beware of those self-limiting beliefs

When I was a small boy, I loved to draw. In school I'd doodle in the margins and I'd sketch the teachers.

At secondary school I thought it was silly to do that in class. So I stopped drawing. But I missed it.

Twenty years ago I enrolled on a couple of classes at Putney School of Art. But I felt out of practice and that my attempts weren't good enough. I told myself, 'I'm no good at drawing'.

Recently I was sorting through the attic and found some of the charcoal drawings from my time at the art school. It was a weird moment, because I didn't really recognize the pictures as mine. I was gobsmacked.

You might tell yourself a story that you are bad at something. But a little bit of distance, and an objective eye, can reveal things to yourself you didn't see before. Self-limiting beliefs can nab you when you're feeling vulnerable and, if you let them, can hold you back from following your passions.

Be careful what you believe about yourself – it just might not be true.

257 Use your story as a compass

Katy Raywood runs an interior design business. She told me about visiting her grandparents' house as a child and how their home decor made an impact. It's why she started her design business.

We all have rich human stories that lie beneath the surface. We've all got tales of overcoming obstacles to follow a dream. Or how your childhood shaped the path you are on today.

Your stories can give you a compass: a path to navigate, somewhere to head towards. To remind yourself, and to tell those around you, why you do what you do.

Know your story and share it with others.

258 Clear your space

This morning on Twitter someone posted a photograph of the office of the *New York Review of Books*. On each desk are piles of books, manuscripts and paperwork. It's a sight to behold!

You might be able to work in a messy space or a cluttered desk, but I can't. I can't get clarity when there's paper piled on top of receipts on top of invoices and so on.

When she's not on the road, my friend Kelly Hoey, author and keynote speaker, works out of her New York apartment. She finds it important to clear her work clutter away every evening so that every day is a fresh start.

She told me she likes to start a day with a clear head, and that means a clear desk.

259 Grab a *hirune* at work

In Japan, a country with a reputation for excessive working hours, some progressive employers are encouraging their employees to take a *hirune*, an afternoon nap. IT services company Nextbeat has a policy that entitles every employee to a 30-minute nap during the working day. Meizen High School in Fukuoka prefecture purportedly saw exam results improve when it recommended students take a nap after lunch.

So grab an afternoon nap and see if it makes a difference to your day.

260 Follow You vs Don't Follow You

Exercise

Take a piece of paper and put a line down the centre, top to bottom, so you now have two columns.

Head the left column 'Not Following Me'. On the right, 'Following Me'.

Take ten minutes to think about the key experiences of your life: friendships, relationships, jobs, holidays and hobbies. Allow them all in, the good and the bad. Consider those that felt very You, and those that didn't.

And now split them between the two columns.

From now on, it's time to focus on putting your attention on the things that only make it into the right column, those that lead you to YOU.

261 Dance your way to health

When Peter Lovatt, the psychologist who studies dance and human movement, was diagnosed with bowel cancer, his doctor told him he'd need to be as fit and strong as possible as he prepared for surgery. Peter knows that a post-operative outcome can be influenced by physical fitness. So he danced daily to get fitter and stronger, both physically and mentally.

Of course it was a worrying time, and he admitted that at times his thoughts went to the worst-case scenario. Peter told me that his daily dance gave him 30 minutes of freedom from these thoughts. He'd turn the music up loud, get lost in the rhythm and escape those concerns that played on his mind.

I'm glad to say Peter got the all-clear. He used dance at every stage of the bowel cancer journey, from diagnosis, through treatment, rehab and recovery. Peter said it saved his body and his mind.

262 Skip a meeting for Mandela!

One morning in August 2007, as I was brushing my teeth, I heard a news item come on the radio: Nelson Mandela was going to be in London that day to unveil a statue of himself.

I felt a tingle up my spine at the mention of his name. This man was an inspiration!

As a teenager I had been a member of the Anti-Apartheid Movement and had marched for his freedom. I had a poster of him on my bedroom wall.

I knew what I needed to do. I made an excuse to Mike – who I was meant to be meeting that morning – and got the tube to Parliament Square.

I knew it was a once-in-a-lifetime opportunity.

What story would you rather tell your grandchildren? That you had a meeting with a bloke called Mike. Or that you went to see Mandela?

263 Fill the house with people and noise

When I'm on holiday, some days I like to have nothing planned. A sense of a blank canvas. Nothing to do. No one to see.

Other days I love to be busy. Seeing friends. Heading from one place to another.

It was a summer's day in August catching up with old friends in Suffolk. We drove over to the coastal town of Orford. We picked up coffee and donuts at the Pump Street Bakery, then ran around with our sticky purchases as we got chased by wasps. As our children explored the castle, my friend Pascal and I walked the grounds, riffing on work ideas. The boys reappeared and played catch, scrambling in the bushes for the lost ball. In the afternoon we walked along quiet country roads to a pub, where we relaxed around a table in the sunshine. The day ended by coming back to ours where we filled the house with people and noise. The kids tucked into tuna pasta bake. We had chicken salad accompanied by a bottle of rosé. There was laughter and lightness.

Good times.

264 Try Emma's 3Ms

Emma Gibbs De Oliveira is the co-founder of Brazilarte, a Brazilian martial arts and dance academy in my hometown. I met Emma when my kids went to the capoeira classes that she runs with her partner.

As a mother of two, one of whom's a toddler, Emma says she needs to be ready to sidestep at any moment.

So she has developed a ritual that helps the daily cogs turn well – Emma's 3Ms: meditation, movement and mind-dump. Emma explains that if she ticks those boxes first thing, she'll start the day well.

So it's ten minutes of meditation. Then 30–60 minutes of movement such as yoga or walking. And then ten minutes of journal writing.

It's a winning combination for her – that three-part daily ritual is what gives her a great day. And if Emma doesn't achieve those basics? She admits the day is a bit touch-and-go!

265 Go for a winter swim in a bobble hat

They're doing it every winter from Helsinki to Ireland. Some wearing wetsuits, others in regular swimsuits and woolly hats.

It was a bitterly cold February morning. As I walked the dog on my local beach there were three women out in the estuary in bobble hats, bouncing about in the sea. 'That was fun!' one of them exclaimed as she waded out, her body a shrimp-pink from the icy water.

In his book *The Other Side of Happiness*, Brock Bastian recalls a study by one of his Phd students in which she surveyed 200 swimmers who took part in a Winter Solstice swim in Tasmania. The student, Laura Ferris, asked participants to rate how painful and how pleasurable they found it.

On average, they rated pain as 4.15 out of 7. They also found it highly pleasurable, rating 6.13 out of 7.

So the pleasure outweighed the pain.

266 Show strangers around your hometown

My old friend Claire Atkinson has a demanding role as a journalist based in New York City. You might expect her to spend her weekends putting her feet up. Not Claire!

Every other weekend she volunteers for Big Apple greeters, a network that matches tourists with walking tour hosts. Originally from Southport, England, Claire's proud of her adopted home city and loves showing tourists around. It might involve sharing breakfast in a diner with an English family or giving German visitors a tour of Union Square Farmers' Market.

The very first person she showed around was a South American lady in her 60s who was staying at the YMCA in Harlem. The lady reciprocated with book and movie recommendations and they still stay in touch today.

When asked what she enjoys so much about it, Claire said that she finds it really stimulating. It gives her something outside her roles as mom and journalist.

Every single occasion is so worth it, she says.

267 Valuing *keyifli*

I love discovering words from other languages that don't have an English translation. Such words tell us about the culture of another country and what they value.

Keyif is one of these words. It's a Turkish word for finding pleasure, feeling blissful or contented in a moment that steps away from the busyness of the day. It's about joy derived from small things. And when you are engaged in activities that are full of *keyif* – that is *keyifli*.

Those simple daily activities. Sitting on a bench enjoying the first coffee of the day. Watching the sunset from my local beach. Sitting in the garden eating a freshly made Greek salad with oregano and extra virgin olive oil.

Tuning into those *keyifli* moments show you that small, fleeting pockets of delight exist in even the most full-on, frantic days. Savour them.

268 Celebrate the wins

It was a late Saturday afternoon in November 2020 and I was listening to Gilles Peterson's radio show on BBC 6 Music. Gilles had been interviewing Elton John and had just played a cover of 'Your Song' that I'd never heard before. It was by Billy Paul and is such a joyous song I cranked up the volume.

That evening the news everyone had been anticipating came through – after days of waiting, it was finally confirmed. A Biden–Harris win for the White House! We had tears of joy. We poured a gin and tonic, put on Billy Paul's 'Your Song' and danced around the kitchen. And then we played it again. And again.

Now I always associate that track with that moment, that feeling of hope against adversity, of positivity of the news and how it felt. Play that song again and I'm snapped straight back into that celebratory mood. Wonderful.

269 Interrupt your teenage hero's soundcheck

A sunny Monday afternoon in March. I was walking down San Jacinto Boulevard in Austin, Texas. As I passed a bar, the windows were open and I could hear the unmistakable sounds of a familiar stripped back guitar and vocals.

'Billy Bragg' I thought to myself.

And then – hang on, that's not a recording – that's Billy Bragg, right here, right now, LIVE in a bar.

I looked through the window and there was the singer songwriter soundchecking.

Billy and I have history. My teenage idol, I interviewed him for BBC local radio while I was a teenager and, in the mid-1980s, went to tens of Bragg gigs around London.

I was 4,950 miles away from home. And here he was in Austin, having just arrived at the South by Southwest festival. I went inside, ordered a Jack Daniels and introduced myself.

The teenage Ian would have been impressed.

270 Follow the good people

In early 1992, 18 months into my dream career in television, the series I was working on didn't get recommissioned. I'd soon be out of a job. What now?

Some of the team I'd worked with were off to start their own business, putting on a music festival. Did I want to join them?

It was never my plan to work on a music festival, but I decided to follow the good people. I liked working with them. We had fun. I learned a lot in those nine months working out of an office in Camden. From Andy I learned how to dream big and have crazy ideas. From John I learned about spreadsheets, to-do lists and how to make bonkers ideas happen. From Mel I learned how a woman juggles her job with a one-month-old baby at her side.

I'm glad I followed the good people.

When you find people you trust, who you know you can do good work with, stick to them like glue!

CHAPTER 10
PUT YOUR LIFE INTO IT

271 Know where you made yourself

In an interview for BBC's *Newsnight* programme, singer-songwriter Róisín Murphy was asked about the cultural importance of the music industry. Róisín explained how important clubs and the music scene had been to her throughout her early life. The places of her youth allowed her to figure out what she was good at and what she might pursue in life.

She said the gigs and clubs she went to as a teenager were where she 'made herself'.

What a wonderful way to describe growing up, and into, music. It suggests she had agency, she actively formed her character and honed her abilities.

Applying that analogy to myself, I made myself in 1986, at the age of 18, as I juggled part-time jobs in radio and music with studying photography.

How about you?

The sports field? In the art class? Your Saturday job?

Where were you made?

272 Do it your way

When I received my first enquiry for coaching, I thought long and hard about the best way of giving people career advice. I knew that I loved being outdoors, I knew that urban adventures fuelled me. And I knew that I found office environments stifling.

So I said to the woman who'd made the enquiry, I'll take you on a three-hour walk.

And fortunately, she said yes. 'Fuel Safari' was born, where I take people on urban walks to help them navigate change in their life.

Giving something a twist with how you want to do things sets you apart, personalizes your offering and helps you be better at what you do. I couldn't get the same results in a café or meeting room – I'm glad I did it my way. The only way I know how.

273 Play Lego

A rainy Sunday with my kids. First we made a model of our favourite coffee shop. Next we made our own version of a Winnebago. And then a container ship.

As I revealed in Idea #136, I love Lego. There are no limits to what you can make – just your imagination.

There's never been a minute spent playing with it that I haven't enjoyed. To be honest, I need very little encouragement. I could happily rummage through a crate of bricks now and make something.

There is something wonderful about it. It's like a game of improvisation. What can you make with a set number of bricks and wheels?

Apparently there are 62 Lego bricks for each person on earth. That's a lot of pieces to get stuck down the planet's sofas.

274 Shine a light and celebrate motherhood

Each of her black and white images is a strong and beautiful portrait of motherhood, such as of a mother cradling her baby as she's seated on a stool, her toddler enclosed in a hug.

This is the Women Body Project, a series of images shared on Instagram by photographer Sarah Barlow (@livingatno.56).

Sarah's intention is to change the narrative around women, particularly mothers of babies and young children, and to challenge the notions around beauty and perfection that place unwarranted pressures upon them. Sarah told me that she seeks to peel back the layers and explore the vulnerabilities mothers often feel they need to hide, and capture and share those with others. Her images enable women to see their true selves afresh, through a new lens, and to celebrate their bodies as well as what it means to be a mother.

With often only a stool as a prop, the intention is for these images to be as raw and honest as possible. The women in the portraits say they feel empowered and seen in a way they haven't felt seen before.

They can ask: this is me, do you see me now?

275 Dine alone

As soon as I stumbled upon Sluizer on Amsterdam's Utrechtstraat I could see it was special. Huge glass windows reach up to a high ceiling. Dark brown floorboards, panelling to waist height beneath white walls. Waiting staff in their monochrome uniforms. Tea lights create a sense of intimacy. At some tables sat couples, at another, a long table of friends.

I took my seat in the middle of the dining floor, on the edge of a raised section. I felt like I was sitting on a stage, but not as the actor or performer but as the audience. An audience of one.

Instantly I felt a number of emotions. A sense of contentment washed over me. I felt at peace.

One of life's biggest pleasures is eating out. And to do so alone is a luxury and a privilege. Being there by myself added to its special-ness. It was like appreciating a piece of art or piece of theatre being able to be 100 per cent dedicated to it.

There was no one to distract me from the experience, where I could taste everything carefully and mindfully, and savour every moment.

276 Nurture your workplace rituals

It was on the second floor of an uninspiring office building just north of the Marylebone flyover. Just an average boardroom with sliding glass doors to an open plan office.

There were no funky furnishings, just a plain old magnolia-painted room. But still, that room was the beating heart of the company I worked at in the 1990s.

And what made this room special were the two rituals that took place inside it.

Every Wednesday morning at 8.30am we'd get together in that room for an all-hands meeting. We'd talk about what was on our minds and what we were up to. It was like taking the pulse of the company.

We'd all get back in that room once a month for First Friday Drinks. There would be bowls of crisps and nuts, bottles of wine and beer. We'd sit back, chat about our week and relax. We'd talk about personal stuff.

Those rituals were our glue at the company.

277 Know when to switch off

For many of us, 'work' is no longer just a place we go to anymore. Work doesn't stay in the building when you leave for the day. Your office lives in your pocket, your home and apartment. You're always accessible. The challenge? How are you able to literally – and metaphorically – switch off?

Even when you're meant to be relaxing and using your phone for leisure, like searching for tracks on Spotify or to catch up on the news, it's too easy to click on the mail icon and see what's in your in-box. And then you might read it or reply to it. Even though it could wait until the morning. Phones are great, but are insidious and have been designed to keep us hooked. So be ruthless if you have to.

Set an app to go offline; be ruthless at night and set it to 'do not disturb'.

278 Fix it, don't chuck it

There's a wonderful product that we always have in our fridge. It's not for eating or drinking. It's Sugru. A brightly coloured, flexible putty that sets on contact to air, you can use it to fix broken objects and hack handy ideas around the house. Repairing a joint on our laundry rack. Making a little edge for a cabinet shelf to keep bottles in place.

Tossing out stuff to end up in landfill isn't the solution, so being able to mend things simply and cheaply is a winner.

Sugru's the invention of Jane Ní Dhulchaointigh and was born out of a eureka moment she had while a student at the Royal College Of Art.

When I visited her HQ in east London, Jane told me that growing up on a farm in rural Ireland helped shape her business idea. She grew up in a household where home-made was the preferred option for a lot of things. Here's to her invention, encouraging a new generation of consumers to repair items instead of throwing them away.

279 Pass the good vibes

It was a Friday morning at the end of a busy week. A one-line email came in from Nick. 'The perfect way to start a Friday morning,' it said, and accompanying it was a YouTube link.

I hit the link, pressed play and turned up my speakers.

It was 'Mr Blue Sky' by The Electric Light Orchestra.

I must admit, it did make my Friday morning go with a swing... but more than that, how nice of Nick to think of me. He'd played it and enjoyed it – he'd passed the good vibes to me.

I then sent the link to my friend.

And hopefully she passed it on too…!

280 Be hope-full

Behaviour is infectious. You know that when you're grumpy, by the end of the day it'll have passed to your colleagues, team members, partners, children.

Over the last few years there's been a lot to worry about. It might take a bit more of an effort to be optimistic and positive. When you choose, however, to be HOPE-full – full of hope rather than worry – it makes a big difference not only to your own mindset and outlook, but to those you live with and work with.

Let's spread that hope around. Even smiling at a stranger as you walk down the street or queue for your coffee can start off a tiny wave of optimism with others.

281 Keep your emotional bandwidth broad

In his book *The Other Side of Happiness*, Brock Bastian says that being happy is not just about pleasure. He says that in order to find happiness, you need to embrace a more fearless approach to living. Because if you look to reduce your pain, the problem is it can narrow what he describes as your emotional bandwidth. You might experience fewer troughs but also fewer peaks. It is your pain that provides an anchor for your pleasure, they are the experiences that ground us as humans.

So keep that emotional bandwidth broad, accept the highs and the lows to give you a fuller, more rounded life and outlook.

282 Pin it

When Madeleine Albright was Secretary of State in President Clinton's administration, she liked to sport a pin on her jacket lapel, depending on her mood. On good days she wore butterflies and balloons. On bad days she wore carnivorous animals and spiders.

I discovered this anecdote from Stanford professor Jennifer Aaker, author of *Humor, Seriously*. Jennifer writes how the Secretary of State used her sense of humour to defuse tensions and build connections: when Albright was at an important international meeting and ambassadors would ask how she was, she would respond with 'Read my pin'.

Even at one of the highest levels of office, Albright drew on her own particular sense of humour during the most serious kind of business, helping her build relationships and conduct international diplomacy in a way that was true to her.

283 Walk around with your eyes open

My friend asked me: you're always going to interesting bars and restaurants, do you have an app where you find them?

An app? Yes, it's called open your eyes!

In Southwark my wife and I walked down Redcross Way, admired an old building I'd passed many times and saw it now housed a Portuguese restaurant. We went inside and had a perfect lunch.

In Liverpool, the first time I'd visited in over 20 years, I walked around following my nose. Reaching a crossroads, I thought, which way now? I saw a bar on the corner. It was called 'Sound'. I walked in. Curtis Mayfield 'Move On Up' was playing. Perfect.

We were in Paris for a few days with the boys. It was our first night and we hadn't researched anywhere for dinner. The children were tired, it was starting to rain. I was about to make a left turn and then, at the last minute, I decided to check out that place on the corner. Café Petite. That was the one. What an amazing night that was.

Maybe our eyes are the best app there is!

284 Have an impromptu garden party

Aren't some of the best experiences in life when a bunch of human beings get together in one place and gather?

One evening in the summer of 2020, we'd been down to the beach for a swim. A number of our friends were there with their kids. At the time, we were in one of the UK's lockdowns. We hadn't got together with people for a while. The rules were that we couldn't have visitors in our house, but we could invite people into our garden.

So we asked our friends back to ours for a sundowner. I lit a fire, put on some music and made a jug of Aperol Spritz.

It was just the perfect couple of hours, sitting around the fire. My friend Dan said it was like our own little festival. It was unplanned and we made do with what we could.

285 Eat together at work

Did you know that the word 'company' derives from the Italian *con panio* – people eating together?

And as I walked into Jamie Oliver's company HQ one lunchtime that derivation was clear to see. Straight ahead was a serving counter where two chefs were plating up vegetable curry. A line of people waiting to be served. And walking around chatting to colleagues, there's the man himself – Jamie.

When I worked in an office, most people tended to eat their lunch 'al desko', grabbing a sandwich or salad and carrying on working. Here at Jamie Oliver's north London HQ, the communal lunch is at the heart of the culture. The ritual started when leftovers from the test kitchen and photo shoots were shared out with colleagues.

Eating together has other benefits too. When Google studied the characteristics of perfect teams, it found that the most productive employees were those who rotated dining companions. Google has caféterias in its offices in the hope its employees will make new connections.

286 Always be on time

If you're looking for a hack to guarantee better results in your life try this:

Turn up on time.

That's it? Yes!

Yet I have worked with so many people in my career who didn't get this right.

A radio producer who was still editing his documentary while a courier waited for 30 minutes outside.

A bloke who consistently turned up late to every meeting I ever arranged with him.

It's not just discourteous. It's going to screw up your day too. All that unnecessary stress about whether you're going to miss your train, or be delayed for your other appointment, or get home too late to say goodnight to your kids. It's a simple but effective hack. If you want a less stressed day, give yourself a head start. Leave early. Arrive early. That way, you'll always be on time.

287 Try bite-sized reading sessions

Recharging during the day, not only at the end of the day or on a weekend, is a key component of a good day for Kelly Hoey.

Even during a busy day at work in her New York apartment, Kelly ensures she disengages from work between online calls. Rather than default to checking email, she likes to have a book of short stories to dip into. Or she'll walk down to collect the mail from the lobby of her apartment, walk around the block or run an errand. For her it's all about paying attention to her focus and energy, and giving herself mini breaks where she can.

288 Your energies waver, and that's OK

I have a professional reputation as someone who gives out positive energy. When I give a talk or take a business leader on one of my 'walk & talks', part of my value is getting people fired-up!

But of course it's not sustainable being like that all the time. I don't have the energy for that.

I can't be like that all day, every day.

It's only natural that your energies ebb and flow. You can't be up all the time. Sometimes you'll feel unstoppable and other times you'll need some time out.

Make peace with your need for peace. Know that in order to be your most energized, you'll need periods of quiet.

289 Ditch the keys

Sam Dixon Brown used to carry around a huge bunch of keys – for his business, home and car. He told me those keys were like trophies of his success and importance. After all Sam, along with his wife Charlie, ran a successful, award-winning local wine shop at the top of my road.

Yet while Sam enjoyed the challenge of entrepreneurship, he wasn't fulfilled. He was constantly busy and always thinking about work. So Sam and Charlie did something radical. They sold the business, their home and all their possessions. They loved wine but they'd missed travelling. Now they live nomadically, moving around wherever takes their fancy. When I spoke to him he was in Dubrovnik, Croatia.

He's learned something contrary to what he used to think: that a simpler life has a lot more to offer. He's found he needs very little to be content and happy. He doesn't put any pressure or expectations on himself.

To Sam now, that big bunch of keys symbolizes all the responsibilities that were weighing him down. Success these days is living without pressure, having the freedom to purely do things on his own terms and taking each day as it comes.

290 Plan for the week ahead

Kelly Hoey, author of *Build Your Own Dream Network*, tells me that every Sunday at 6pm she has an alert on her phone: 'First-things-first for the week ahead' which prompts her to think about what's coming up.

Kelly says having this reminder helps her prioritize, get focused and make sure there are no surprises. What does she need to prepare for? What has she forgotten about? What does she need to cancel or confirm?

I second Kelly – I'd much rather think about those things at the end of a weekend than deal with them in a rush as the week gets underway.

And having diarized time to devote to it means Kelly has a commitment to getting it done.

291 Put your life into it

In 2021 artist Damien Hirst revealed his latest work: a collection of one hundred canvases of psychedelic cherry blossom.

In an interview with the *Financial Times*, Hirst spoke about how alive he felt during the painting process. He'd climb up a ladder, with his paint mixed in buckets, and then he'd throw the paint from a distance onto the canvas. He said it was like he was putting his life into it – all that energy of life caught in the paint.

That sense of putting your life into something – whether a hobby, a passion or just how you spend your days – leaves a mark.

Putting your life into something is more than just turning up the energy dials. It's pouring your essence, your story and life lessons onto that canvas. It's an intensity of purpose and action that says this really matters, I care about it.

292 Notice new things on old walks

A Mexican restaurant in the Mission District.

Plant pots outside a front door in Potrero Hill.

Stunning architecture in Noe Valley.

These are some of the images of San Francisco that my friend Karen Wickre – who we met in Idea #94 – has been sharing on Instagram along with the hashtag #dailywalk.

When lockdown hit in March 2020, a dear friend of Karen's was dying from pancreatic cancer. Karen decided a good way to keep vigil was to take a photograph on her daily walks and send those to him. Barry was a great flaneur. The two friends used to take long walks together, talking about everything from politics to relationships.

After Barry passed away, Karen decided to continue taking her photos on her daily walks with her dog Zuzu. Each time she aimed to see something new, or something old in a fresh way. Maintaining her creative Instagram habit helps her tune into what she's drawn to, and to keep an eye out for things she's not noticed before. It keeps her walking on through the city, and remembering her friend and how much she enjoyed their time together.

293 Go for a bike ride to beat your post-lunch slump

Watch out for what you put in your work calendar between 2.30 and 3.30pm.

A report by *Medical Daily* found that 2.55pm was a low energy point for UK workers. It tends to be around now that you get that post-lunch slump a lot of us are likely familiar with.

You've seen it, or are aware of flagging energy levels, in workspaces and convention centres. On returning to the auditorium after a lunch break the room feels stuffy and everyone looks like they could do with a nap.

How can you counter that slump?

After attending one of my 'More Good Days at Work' sessions, company founder Jane told me her action point was to take a 3pm bike ride. She felt it was the ideal way of avoiding that dip. Even better – she always has her best ideas on her bike.

294 Turn a routine into a ritual

Psychotherapist Esther Perel explains how routines and rituals play an important role in our lives, especially relationships. In a livestream on her YouTube channel, Esther explains how routines help us create structure and predictability, a necessity during the good times, the hard times, and life's big transitions.

We each have the chance to turn a routine into a ritual. Rituals are routines elevated by creativity, driven by intention and meaning.

So laying the table for dinner is a routine. But laying the table with candles and flowers is a ritual. It's about what you do every day versus what you can do to add meaning. Turning an average meal into a special night.

Routines might be boring but rituals are essential in every relationship. There's a subtle but essential difference. I've started to think about how I can turn some of our family routines into rituals, to make a positive difference for everyone.

295 Take 10,000 steps a day

There's not that much I measure in life.

I don't record every run or bike ride on an app on my phone.

I don't care whether yesterday's seafront run was faster than last week's.

But there is one thing I track every day via my smartwatch – and that is how many steps I'm taking.

I make sure I do my target of 10,000 steps.

So when it pings to let me know I have hit my target, that's a good sign.

And when it says 'you've been inactive for an hour' I know it's time to get up.

296 Make a soup for a winter's lunch

A winter's lunchtime. It's cold, wet and miserable outside.

On days like these there's something special about a warming soup.

This is one of my favourites. I find it really mindful to make.

- Slice up three leeks and fry for 20 minutes in butter.
- Chunk up three medium potatoes and throw those in. Cook for five more minutes.
- Add 1.5 litres stock.
- Throw in some parmesan rinds.
- Stir.
- Leave to simmer for 40 minutes. Remove the rinds. Blend, season and stir.
- Sprinkle some parmesan.

Thank you for the recipe Nigel Slater. It's not just the eating, I love the joy in the making.

297 Choose an unusual space for a meeting

On Twitter, Sarah Drinkwater shared a photograph of a wonderful location for a meeting she'd been to. It was a small fishing cabin in the village of Grundsund on the Swedish west coast. This was the scene of a meeting with Data 4 Change, where Sarah is a board member.

I can think of some memorable locations over the years. A project meeting around David Hieatt's candle-lit dining table on his farm in west Wales. A fire was lit. Fresh coffee was poured. A dog snoozed by my feet (that was a good one).

I'm all for having meetings outside of conventional spaces. Where you have meetings might just be as important as what's covered within them. Location can make a big difference to your engagement and ultimately what can be achieved.

298 Unhurry

One way I make time to slow down from the busy day is to grab the dog lead, put on my headphones and go out for an afternoon walk while I listen to a podcast. One podcast I stumbled upon seemed rather apt. It was called 'Unhurried' and was made by professional facilitator Johnnie Moore. Johnnie says that our default culture is to be forever rushing and over-stimulated. Yet you've got the opportunity to tap into a more relaxed form of creativity and appreciate more of what you have instead of spending less time chasing after things that you don't.

Listening to 'Unhurried' reinforced the changes I needed to make, to lessen the urge to rush from one thing to another.

299 A sweet spot is worth the wait

In the middle of a business downturn, things weren't going so well. Then I was offered a substantial contract to work with a woman I really love working with. Initially I thought, great, I can earn some much-needed revenues.

But I turned it down. Because I realized that what I'd be doing for her wasn't in my sweetspot. I always want to do and be my absolute best for a client. When I'm passionate and interested about something, then I know I can give my all.

Turning down a project that's not right gives space for other, more suitable propositions to come along. Which is exactly what happened a few months later.

300 Share a story and share a bond

At the beginning of the year Paul from Seattle sent me an email. He had reached out after attending an online talk I'd given.

In the talk I'd spoken about my teenage dream to work in broadcasting and how, at the age of 18, I'd interviewed my hero Billy Bragg. In his email, Paul wrote that when he was a teenager, the musician had been his hero too. He'd even once wooed a potential girlfriend with one of Billy's songs (it worked – she agreed to go out with him).

Personal stories have such power to connect you with others, uniting you beyond business, going behind the job title and direct to the human being.

It was a lovely moment to receive Paul's email about our shared interest. We were simply two people, thousands of miles apart, uniting over a story.

CHAPTER 11
JUST HAVE A DAY

301 Just have a day

My focus on having a good day is not about airbrushing out the bad days. Everyone has bad days.

Sometimes life can feel challenging, overwhelming, unnavigable. Looking too far ahead is like being on a ship at sea when you can't see what's over the horizon. And at times like those I've found it's better just to take life day-by-day. Just to focus on the here and now.

And to acknowledge how you're feeling rather than fight it.

Emily's my therapist friend (we met her in Idea #26). When we talked about the notion of a 'good day', she challenged me on it. She wondered whether a good day – a whole, well-rounded, fulfilling day – might have to have elements of contrast in order for us to notice the good bits.

Light complements shade. This interrelationship of lows and highs makes up the human condition. How can you know you're in the light, if you've not experienced the dark? That messy array of feelings gives life meaning.

So if you can't have a good day, perhaps just have a day.

302 Eat culture for lunch

If you worked at Olivetti typewriter company in the 1950s you would have had a two-hour lunch break. One hour to eat food and one hour to eat culture. The head of the company, Adriano Olivetti, thought it was important for his employees to soak up knowledge and information from different worlds. In this extended break, workers could go to a library, watch a lecture or music recital.

Mr Olivetti attributed innovations in typewriters to that simple idea. By encouraging a curious and intellectually stimulating approach, it led to greater innovation and increased productivity. The company expanded significantly and branched out into making a wide range of products.

303 Tune in to a moment in flow

It's January 2018. I'm in Leeds, a city I've had a love affair with since I lived here as a student. I have checked out of my hotel, I've had a superb coffee at La Bottega Milanese and I'm walking down Headrow listening to 'There Is A Light That Never Goes Out' on my headphones.

I arrive at the BBC Yorkshire building where I've come to run a workshop/ lecture with a roomful of journalists. I love it. Pacing up and down. Animated. Passionate. Getting them laughing. Knowing that what I say matters as they scribble down notes.

As I walked away I realized something – that this is me in my element.

Those moments when you feel in flow are so powerful.

They are a gift from above.

Feeling invincible, being happy. That energy. Walking tall.

Whatever you're doing and experiencing when you feel like this – is what you are meant to be doing.

304 Know what magnifies you

Maria Popova's Brainpicker site is a regular font of wisdom where she discusses and articulates ideas from across the creative, scientific and spiritual spectrum.

One idea of hers I particularly love is her encouragement to find those things that magnify you. Whether it's a person, a particular idea or a book you love – what is it that enhances you, makes you bigger, lights you up?

It's a clear and powerful call to help you know what's in, know what's out.

I know the people who sap me. I could write that list now. And even in thinking of those names, I feel hunched over.

And then BAM!! The people who magnify me, it's like a bolt of lightning, a huge flash of white light. I am walking tall. I am invincible.

The difference is palpable.

305 Walk on the beach

The Barcelona Institute for Global Health ran a survey where in the first week they asked participants to spend 20 minutes walking along Barcelona's beach front. During the second week they were asked to walk through the city streets. The participants reported that taking just a 20-minute walk on the beach boosted their mood and mental health. Probably not that surprising really.

I'm very lucky that I have a beach five minutes from my front door. It's not a soft, sandy one that stretches for miles, but still – it's a beach.

The beach is a place for wandering, wondering, mulling things over, getting the cobwebs blown about, de-stressing with the kids after dinner, a place to talk through worries.

I don't need a study to tell me this, but sometimes I might need a reminder to get those sandy shoes on and get crunching that grainy sand.

306 Be like Stevie

He wanted to shake hands and say hello to everybody in the room. Even the 22-year-old carrying the tripod.

Which is how I came to meet Stevie Wonder.

It was in the penthouse suite at the Conrad Hotel, Chelsea Harbour. We were there to film an interview with him. My role was the least glamorous. Carry the tripod and take away the Betacam SP tapes afterwards.

Mr Wonder wanted to meet everybody – even the most junior person in the room.

Such a class act. Isn't he lovely…?!

307 Expand your ideas

My experience is that when there are fewer physical constraints in your surroundings, it allows for freer thinking. At the bottom of the road where I live is the Thames estuary. Depending on the tide, there's either a huge expanse of sea or mudflats. And big skies.

This environment of the open skies and estuary landscape that stretches on and up, inspires open thinking. Rain or shine, the view inspires and brings clarity. This landscape by the mouth of the Thames has been described as an 'edgeland', a place of transition that connects the UK to the rest of the world. Giant container ships from the Netherlands and China glide to and from the London Gateway super port; in the autumn flocks of geese from Siberia make their winter home on the estuary's muddy banks. It's a great place to think.

If you want to expand your ideas, remove your physical constraints.

308 Stay true to a life that's you

In 2015, I was offered a job based by Lake Geneva. After 14 years of working solo, I was tempted by the idea of stability. A regular paycheck again. Working for a prestigious company.

Shortly after receiving the offer, I gave a guest lecture at the University of East London. Sitting down for a pizza and Peroni in Pizza Express Stratford afterwards, I was struck by something: this is the path I should be on, standing on stage and energizing others. Not sitting at a desk, however beautiful the location. That lecture, at a location far from the shores of the Swiss lake, had helped me rediscover my purpose.

It was a clarion call – stay true to a work life that's you.

309 Feed your hunger for change

I know myself, I know what I wanted – this is what my friend Sejal told me about relocating to Barcelona. For the creative brand consultant, leaving San Francisco for a new life in Spain was about making time for, and designing a life around, the things she feels are important.

She and her partner sought somewhere more affordable, where they could enjoy a good quality of life, work less, and where she could immerse herself more fully in her art practice, something she'd longed to do since leaving art school.

When she told people she was moving to Barcelona, she'd sometimes hear back 'Oh, I'd love to do that too, but...' and there'd be a reason why they couldn't.

We all have 'buts', Sejal told me. What it comes down to is really tuning in to that desire for change. So she became intentional about it, and focused on ways to make it happen.

310 Drink a mindful cuppa

I love my coffee.

My friend Hugh – who we met in Idea #129 – loves his tea.

(No, it's not the start to an old English nursery rhyme.)

Hugh drinks a lot of tea. But once a day he makes time for a special cuppa. He closes his laptop, and for 15 minutes he'll simply look out of the window and enjoy the taste, be in the moment with no distractions.

He told me he really looks forward to it.

How often do we stop to really notice what we're tasting, rather than just drink it as we power through our to-do lists?

Hugh said that when he mindfully sips his drink, it always feels like a very different cup of tea.

He can taste the difference.

311 Send someone a bag of marbles

When I shared on Instagram the childhood story that I'd swallowed a marble at the age of eight, a good contact of mine, Michael Burne, commented that he too had swallowed a marble when he was eight. What are the chances of that?! Michael was already the founder of an innovative law firm who I really respected, and now it felt like we were members of an exclusive club!

That lunchtime I walked down to our local toy shop, bought a bag of marbles, put a little note on them saying 'Please do not eat' and mailed them to his office in Cardiff.

He appreciated the gesture, posting a photograph of them on Instagram. He even received a comment from a woman in Australia who'd swallowed a marble at eight. There were now three of us ;)

If you too swallowed a marble at eight years old, join our club!

312 Live the *susegad* life

Goa – the region in western India well known for its beaches and laid back vibe.

But there's more to Goa than the tourist websites show you. And at the heart of Goan culture is *susegad* – a sense of feeling relaxed, fulfilled and content. It's about creating habits and routines that lend happiness and calm to your life.

Clyde D'Souza, author of *Susegad: The Goan Art of Contentment*, says living the *susegad* life starts with increasing your awareness and doing things more consciously.

I've yet to visit Goa, but I think we could all benefit from being more content and fulfilled. Here's to the *susegad* life.

313 Follow the sun...

This morning it was an English spring day full of bright sunshine and optimism.

I let the dog out and she headed for her favourite position in the garden, lying in the sun.

And I thought, she's onto something.

Later, I fetched a takeout coffee and headed down to the seafront.

Down on the promenade, I counted 30 or 40 similar souls, some in sunglasses, others with eyes closed, heads tilted towards the sun.

In Northern European countries, sunlight can be a precious commodity. Visit cities like Copenhagen or Amsterdam in the winter, and you'll see people sitting outside cafés, blankets over legs, nursing coffees or glasses of wine, all in a line to be in the best position to feel the sun on their faces.

So when the sun comes, you need to make the most of it, and grab the warmth and light while you can. Darker rainier days will inevitably lie around the corner.

Here comes the sun… follow it!

314 Forgive someone

Most of us have had experiences where we feel wronged by someone. You feel let down or hurt. But walking around with a grudge can bring you down. Would it be possible instead to forgive that person?

Forgiving someone doesn't mean denying yourself that feeling of being hurt. It does mean you can liberate yourself from that weight of feeling so angry about it on a daily basis.

Elise Kalokerinos is a lecturer at the University of Melbourne and an expert in emotion regulation. She says that when you constantly ruminate about something, it can lead to a lessening of wellbeing and raises the chance of illness and poor health.

To forgive isn't to forget, it's to go easy on yourself instead.

315 Track down someone you met 30 years ago and say thanks

When I was ten we went on a family holiday to Wales. In the bed and breakfast where we were staying we met an American family: parents, children and their uncle. We exchanged addresses and the uncle – Richard – used to send us Christmas presents for a few years afterwards.

How thoughtful and generous! We'd only met him briefly.

It was so exciting receiving those annual packages from the United States. One year we received a deluxe edition of Scrabble. The next year, an electronic memory game called Einstein.

From his correspondence we discovered that Richard was a Superior Court Judge for the County of Los Angeles. How cool was that!

About ten years ago I tracked him down online to say thank you for all those wonderful gifts. He was still living in California but it turned out he was soon to visit London. We reunited for drinks at his apartment near Sloane Square. We hadn't seen each other for 30 years, we hadn't even kept in touch, but still we had that shared story. And I still have that deluxe Scrabble set, complete with a rotating board.

316 Hide notes in your family's packed lunches

Before my wife and I were married, when we'd just started living together, I'd often prepare a Tupperware lunch box of leftovers for her to take into the office. And some days I'd tuck into the salad leaves a little note saying something funny. She told me it really made her smile. Then when my kids were small, I sometimes used to do the same, leaving little 'I love you' notes in their lunchboxes.

Like a real-life text message, buried in the lettuce leaves or pasta shells.

317 Experience togetherness

Before March 2020, we had little interaction with most of our neighbours on our street. We'd all go about our daily lives, waving in acknowledgement or dropping in a Christmas card, but no more than that.

But as the world changed, connections were built. Now we stopped to compare notes on availability of groceries locally. Was anyone self-isolating and needed shopping? A WhatsApp group for the street started up. Who could get hold of eggs, or bananas or – most importantly – coffee?!

And in March 2021, on the 12-month anniversary of the first lockdown in the UK, we stood on our doorstep holding candles and shining the torches from our phones.

We waved across at neighbours on balconies and at front gates.

In times of need, we all came together – we were all there for each other when it really mattered.

318 Make someone smile with a voice note

I have strange dreams, often vivid and quite bizarre. One morning I was laughing out loud at the memory of one I'd had the night before. Featuring an old friend of mine and a very strange tattoo.

I thought, I've got to tell him about it!

So – with the laughter in my voice – I hit record on my WhatsApp and sent him a voice message.

When we lead busy lives it can be hard knowing the right time to call someone. You might not fancy a long chat. But with a voice message there's no onus on you to pick up a call. You can play it back at your convenience. It shows the other person you are thinking of them, it's personal.

And on this occasion a text message wouldn't have cut it!

319 Take your surfboard to the office

If you're lucky enough to work for the outdoor clothing company Patagonia, as long as the work gets done, you're able to work flexible hours. At the heart of that rule lies the philosophy of company founder Yvon Chouinard.

In his book *Let My People Go Surfing*, Yvon explains that the company values employees who live rich lives. And when it comes to surfing, he says that a passionate surfer doesn't plan to go next week. You go when the conditions are right.

Here at The Ian Sanders Company, we have a similar philosophy: 'Let our people go swimming.' Ok, it's me and my business partner, who also happens to be my wife. We live and work five minutes from a beach. Here on the Thames estuary you can only swim at high tide so when the tide is in, we down tools and run down for a dip.

You gotta do what you gotta do.

320 Don't be restricted by your own thoughts

My friend David Sloly – who we met in Idea #186 – is like me. He loves the thrill and the challenge of trying new things.

Every year David adds a new string to his bow. Three years ago he tried his hand at stand-up comedy. Last year he started writing a book, getting up at 5.30 every morning to write. He's enjoyed that so much, he's still at it. But this year he told me he wanted more stimulation. So he signed up to an online learning course from Oxford University on Artificial Intelligence. It's a sense of the new that keeps him on his toes.

He wrestles with the complexity of mathematical algorithms, but loves the feeling when he masters it and emerges on the other side with clarity. That gives him a high.

So I asked him, why do you do it? It's about training himself to do things he didn't think he could do. Because when it comes to thinking about what you can do, the only things that restrict you are your own thoughts about it.

321 Get out of your depth

Do you feel safe and comfortable at work? Then, according to David Bowie, you're not working in the right area.

In a clip from the 1997 TV documentary *Inspirations*, David talks about what being a successful artist means to him. His philosophy is applicable I believe to not only musicians and artists, but to any of us – whatever we do – who want to make a difference through our work.

Go further into the water, he says. Go a little out of your depth. And when you feel your feet aren't quite touching the bottom – you're just about in the right place to do something exciting.

322 Scratch an itch

Every few weeks Joel Bukiewicz posts a photograph on his website of a selection of beautiful kitchen knives. They're all handmade by him in his Brooklyn workshop. He doesn't have an order book. He simply posts this message underneath: 'Send me an email if any of these belong to you.' When they're gone, they're gone.

When I met Joel some years ago he explained his craft was borne out of a need to express himself creatively. So he made one knife. He loved it. And he made another. And another.

And then all of a sudden he was a knifemaker.

Sometimes you might overthink what you need to get started.

That you need a grand plan. But actually achievement often comes simply by turning up and getting your hands dirty. In Joel's case, that's literally. Making knives is hard, grubby and painful work. Joel's invested time, blood and sweat scratching his itch. It's making at its most essential and uncomplicated.

323 Go to mountains, moors and heathland

George MacKerron, Senior Lecturer in Economics at the University of Sussex, analysed the habits of more than 20,000 users of his smartphone app Mappiness. He found that people living in the UK report the highest happiness when outdoors and in natural habitats. And in particular, many were happiest when close to mountains, moors and heathland.

Don't despair if you can't get out into nature, even looking out of the window can help. MacKerron cites research that studied the recovery records of patients in a Pennsylvania hospital. Patients whose rooms faced a natural setting received fewer negative comments in nurses' notes and required less medication.

Next time your son or daughter gets a note in their school report saying they daydream out the window too much, perhaps it's time to cut them some slack – they're clearly onto something.

324 Hit 'record' to easily rewind

How can you make sure you capture those special memories and not let them slip through your hands?

When Hugh Garry took his teenage kids on holiday one year, he realized it would probably be the last time they'd all go away together. Sitting on the Khao San Road in Bangkok eating Pad Thai, Hugh had a sense of something: that this here, right now, was going to be an especially important memory. Something he would always look back on.

So he hit his mental record button. He looked around him and took in the scene. He listened to the sounds. He noticed the taste of the food. And how it smelt.

Because he paid attention to that moment, that memory today is as if he hits a rapid rewind. Even in retelling the story to me all these years later, Hugh said the smells and sounds came flooding back.

325 Do what makes your heart beat faster

Around the ages of 17 and 18, I regularly used to make speeches at family gatherings. I felt in my element standing up in front of everyone making them laugh. That confidence continued into my time at college – when I was active in the Student Union – and lasted through the first ten years of my working life where I was always up on stage with a microphone.

But something happened. I'm not sure what exactly, but I lost that confidence. I started to fear public speaking. Just an email landing in my in-box asking me to give a talk would get my heart racing.

So I began making excuses why I couldn't make a speech and I shied away from the limelight.

But after a few years I wanted to overcome all that. I knew I'd once loved it, and I wanted to do so again. I thought to myself, I can run away from this or I can run towards it.

You know what I chose? I ran towards it. It took some time and practice but I love it again. It makes my heart beat faster, but it's with excitement, not fear.

326 Walk in someone else's shoes.

How can we better understand those we work with? How can we see the world from their point of view?

A few months after starting her new role at a global telecommunications company, my friend Sally Croft spent her Monday morning up a 160-feet bell tower at the top of a cathedral. She was in a senior office-based role and knew that the best way to get in the mindset of the 4,000 field engineers who work for the company was to walk in her colleagues' shoes. Or more accurately, prerequisite special-issue steel capped boots and hard hat!

So she climbed up the steep narrow bell tower staircase to share in the engineer's experience. Watching him perform his tasks at the top meant she could see first-hand his dedication and professionalism. Reading a report about the engineers could never have replicated how it felt being there in person.

327 Make an impromptu trip to the cinema

I'd wanted to see Steve McQueen's film *Widows* for some time. But it wasn't playing in my home town.

But then I'd just finished a meeting in Regent Street, and had an idea.

Checking cinema listings on my phone, I reckoned I could just make it to the 12.30 screening at The Curzon in Soho.

It was a real treat, going to the cinema in the middle of the working day, and I loved the film.

But what made it even more of a treat? What made it so memorable?

I was the only one there – it turned out it was a screening just for me! Now that was a good day!

328 Feel small in the universe

You walk into a cathedral. You look at the mountains from the aeroplane window. And let out a 'wow...'

Having a sense of awe – that state of being amazed by overwhelming beauty or so taken with a scene you are dumbstruck – can bring lots of positives to your daily life. In Idea #84 I showed how people who look out for awe every day increase their happiness. In his book, *Awestruck*, psychologist Jonah Paquette draws on studies that prove awe-inducing experiences boost mood. When you are overcome with awe, he says, you experience a 'small self' – your ego is reduced, and you become more aware of your surroundings, other people and the universe at large.

Not only is awe a pleasant feeling, it can decrease stress as well as increase life satisfaction and increase generosity.

329 Look out from the top

Where you stand can alter your perception of the world.

A January morning ten years ago I was travelling west on the District Line, worrying about an uncertain year ahead of me, unsure how I might bring my business back to health.

I emerged from the tube station into a cold, sunlit Sloane Square around 10am. I had 30 minutes spare before my meeting. I took the escalator to the top floor of the Peter Jones department store and sat in the window with my coffee. Looking across the rooftops I felt my mindset and outlook shift. Up here I genuinely felt differently to how I'd done down below.

I looked out to the majestic dome of the Royal Albert Hall, turned to look west towards the iconic Trellick Tower then east to Centrepoint and, in that moment, I felt the world was my oyster. This vista – and all those ungrabbed opportunities out there – are all there for exploring. Mine for the taking!

Life was good, I said to myself.

To elevate your thoughts, sometimes you just need to rise up.

330 Just do it!

An early morning in August walking the dog along the seafront. The tide was high and as we approached the shoreline, the sun came out.

I'd love a swim, I told my wife.

But I had no swimming trunks, no towel.

Go on, my wife urged me, 'Just do it!'

So I looked up and down the path. No one was close by, so I whipped off my jeans and t-shirt and ran in.

It was a truly 'no f***s given' moment, swimming out across the still water.

And it was all the better for it being unplanned. A truly life-affirming experience.

CHAPTER 12

IF IT MAKES YOU FEEL GOOD, DO MORE OF IT

331 Know yourself

There are 39.7 million posts on Instagram with the hashtag #goodday. And yes – quite a few of them feature sunsets, beaches and cocktails.

My friend Emily is a psychotherapist who works with people who are struggling, and part of her work is with young people and students. Emily sees first-hand the effects of social media and the unfavourable comparisons we can often make. If your notion of a good day doesn't match the one that everybody else *seems* to be having, it can lead to feeling that you are lacking in some way. It can result in anxiety and self-doubt.

And, of course, on Instagram it largely shows people putting on their best face. What's going on behind the scenes might be entirely at odds with the image they're presenting.

Emily cautions that social media can be a major contributor to having a bad day, especially if you are not in a great place already. So if you're not feeling great, perhaps stay off Instagram, and instead focus on what a good day looks like for YOU.

It starts with knowing, and being comfortable, with yourself. It's nothing to do with anyone else.

332 Just be in your body

Many of the ideas in this book involve external stimuli to have a good day: taking a journey, sitting in a café, listening to music.

But there'll be times when having a good day requires the stripping away of exterior elements, to simply be.

As I suggested in Idea #146, improving your day might not be about adding a new element, but about subtracting from it instead.

Jerry Colonna lives on a farm 12 miles out of Boulder, Colorado. On a video call from his home – where I could clearly hear wonderful birdsong out his window – he told me he'll start the day sitting in the backyard with his coffee watching the sunrise. It's just what Jerry needs to focus his mind: he can gaze across to the snow-capped peaks, enjoy the peace and simply be in the moment. It's what a good day looks like for him: quiet, connection with the land and being in his body.

333 Stop chasing the 'if onlys'

Sometimes it feels like we go through life waiting on a future that might never happen.

I did it myself. I said I would be happy in my self-employed work life if only I could find a company who would hire me for three days a week. I set my heart on that goal – it remained on my horizon for years not months!

The trouble was, I couldn't make it happen. And because I couldn't make it happen I felt dissatisfied. What if I never pull off the plan? I'll never be satisfied.

Then I had a moment of clarity. I just needed to get on and live.

I changed my mindset and resolved to live more in the Now. To appreciate the present and not chase a future built on 'if onlys'.

I stopped chasing the future – which by its very nature is always out of reach – and started living the present, appreciating what I have in front of me right now.

334 It's the journey, not the destination

One way of approaching life is to put your foot down on the accelerator, hit 100mph and get to your destination – career success, money, recognition, goals – as fast as you can.

And for the first nine or ten years of my career that was my philosophy. Until I had my crash.

It forced me to slow down, take it easy. When I did that I discovered the joy in the journey. I was no longer rushing over to end up somewhere. Instead I have meandered the back roads, meeting interesting people, soaking up wonderful stories, having experiences that feed my soul along the way.

I'm glad I was forced to pull over from the fast lane, where I could cruise and stop and take time to look around. It's a much better view… life doesn't go by in a blur ;)

After all, constantly fixing your sights on the horizon risks missing out on what's right in front of you.

335 Make a pack of 'What makes me tick' cards

Exercise

I have a pack of pocket-sized orange cards that are really special to me. On one side of around 20 of these cards I've written a word or phrase with a Sharpie. Each of the words means something – they are the qualities that I value in my life and reflect who I am. My essence.

I call this pack, 'What makes me tick'.

I have the cards in front of me now. I hadn't looked at them for a while, and what's interesting is that they seem to reflect the ideas in this book!

If I get lost, and wonder where I'm headed in life, I get the deck of cards out to remind myself what I'm all about.

I use a pack of Artefact cards but you can use anything. It's an idea I got from a friend – thanks Lizzie.

Give it a go and write down the values and qualities that define you. See how you get on.

336 Be like the stake

Every morning I walk along the beach and pass a tall wooden stake in the mud.

It's almost like a totem. Once used to moor boats, it now has no particular use, but it remains there, a constant fixture on the scene. Whether at low tide in the mud, high tide in the swell of the estuary, in still waters or stormy, come rain or shine, during winter or summer, in the morning and at night – it stands tall, whatever gets thrown at it.

I always take strength from this unremarkable landmark. Over the years I've come to just sit and look out at it. It's strangely comforting when I'm having a difficult day. I'd bring my sons down here when they were toddlers, just to hang out.

I can see it now as I write these words, a silent guardian, steady and firm.

337 Persevere

The first time I applied for a place on my university degree course, I was rejected. I was accepted a year later, once I had some work experience under my belt.

The first time I pitched my book idea to a publisher, they said 'no thanks'. I returned a few months later with a snappier title and a pitch via a YouTube video. The same company I'd originally approached gave me a book deal.

The first time I approached an editor at the *Financial Times*, he said he wasn't looking for new writers. I kept in touch and got a meeting with him a few months later, securing the first of a regular series of articles. Thanks for persevering, my soon-to-be editor Ravi said, as we sat down for coffee.

Sometimes it's a case of luck, of right time, right place. Sometimes, you've got to keep knocking.

338 Salami slice it

When life or your to-do list feels overwhelming, try salami slicing it.

One task at a time. One step at a time.

Salami slicing makes the overwhelming more realistic.

It's like writing and editing this book.

Writing and editing a 55,000 word book sounds daunting.

But when it's just one line that follows another, that follows another. That's manageable.

Take it slice by slice.

339 Look for inspiration in the food market

Howard Schultz is the founder of Starbucks. When he returned to Starbucks as CEO in 2008 he convened a meeting with the leadership team in Seattle. The brand had lost its way and the soul of the company was at risk. Schultz knew they needed to put the customer back at the heart of everything they did. At the end of the first day, the team split up and immersed themselves in Seattle's food market. They were told to observe the food stalls and report back.

At a cheese counter, Schultz was struck by the expertise of the woman behind the counter. She was so knowledgeable and passionate about the product even though she'd only worked there a few months. She put it down to having great training.

That chance encounter inspired an exercise inside Starbucks, where 7,000 stores were closed for 3½ hours so baristas could be retrained to make the perfect espresso.

Immersing yourself in the world around you doesn't only make a difference to your wellbeing and mood – it also fuels ideas and innovation.

340 Have a positive mindset at work

When your work life is full-on, it's important for you to tune in to how you can give yourself a boost and alleviate some of the pressure. My friend Sally Croft – who we met in Idea #326 – has a senior role at a global organization where her days are often full of back-to-back meetings. To give her a buffer, she bookends her day with outside activity, starting the day with a walk with her dog Lily and ending it riding her ebike around the Surrey hills.

These activities fulfil her need to celebrate aliveness – recognizing the fragility of life and to be grateful for her health and quality of life.

And if she can't always get outside to have those moments of aliveness, she'll look for ways mentally to do it. For Sally this means always trying to stay positive. She told me that misery likes company – it's so much easier to spend time on what's going wrong. As a leader, she likes to encourage her team to remind themselves of the good things and to celebrate success, as well as looking at challenges with a positive mindset.

341 If it makes you feel good, do more of it

Over the years Hugh and I would meet at Shoreditch House, a members club in east London.

Once, he told me, he'd gone to the gym and then headed up to the top floor to base himself there for a while. If sunny, he'd sit outside by the rooftop pool. He liked it so much, he set his morning routine so he'd do it every day.

Making a choice to do something starts with a simple action, and for Hugh that's being finely tuned to how he's feeling at any given time. If he's feeling good – he does more of whatever he's doing. And if he's not feeling good, he doesn't repeat the activity. It's a simple thing, but how often do you really notice what you feel, and then act on it?

Hugh and his partner Rikki had been thinking about moving from London to Ibiza. In 2020 they tested it out by living there for three months, during which Hugh felt the best he'd ever felt in his life. It was an easy decision for Hugh and Rikki – Ibiza's where they want to be.

342 Combat distractions

Paul Benney runs DMY, an online music platform and artist services company. His best days at work are those when he stays focused on the tasks in hand and avoids getting sidetracked.

Paul admits distraction is a challenge. Social media is essential for Paul's business and he needs to check it constantly. But with it of course comes all those other shiny, interesting posts that vie for attention.

To combat distraction, Paul employs different strategies depending on what needs to get done. He'll turn his phone off, or even just flip it over so he can't see the screen. He also deletes apps that he finds distracting, keeping only those ones that are actually useful for his productivity. Or he might hide apps in folders away from his main phone screen. And having notifications switched off is a must. One thing he says he finds helpful when doing head-down work is having only the browser he's working in open.

Concentrated, deep work is hard for most of us these days. Being aware of whatever's standing in your way is the first step to being more productive.

343 Direct your own movie

An email newsletter from Allison Schultz, a coach at the leadership development firm Reboot, landed in my in-box. In it Allison talks about the theme of becoming the director of your life.

I love that concept! When you're the director of your life, you call the shots.

Only you know all the ingredients required to have a good day.

You know what makes you most fulfilled, gets you in your element and stirs you so you're rocking and rolling.

Put yourself in the director's chair. What scenes are coming next? Who is in the starring roles? What will end up on the cutting room floor? This is the movie of your life. You get to choose.

What life would you like to create for yourself?

344 Buy something for Rob

I was walking down a London street when I walked past a homeless guy sitting on the pavement. He smiled at me. I smiled back.

I stopped and turned back.

We might feel conflicted about how best to help the homeless. Organizations are great to support, but the advice not to give money to individuals is hard to abide by.

That morning though I could satisfy my desire to help. On his piece of cardboard was written: 'Clean socks, underwear, food needed. Thank you.'

I stopped and he told me his name was Rob. He didn't want money, he just needed supplies. What can I get you? I asked. He told me he needed some underpants.

So that's what I got him.

345 Leave the zone of straight edges

We spend so much of our working lives on tablets, laptops and smartphones. But is that the best way of approaching creativity? Who said that staring at a silver or black rectangle was going to be the best way to generate ideas?

My friend Lizzie Everard, a creative director living in Bristol, certainly doesn't believe it is. When it's a sunny day Lizzie heads off to an environment full of curves, greenery and organic matter: Plot 41 – her allotment. She'll take along her notebook and storyboard pens and sit on a bench, just taking it all in. She likes that here things happen outside your control. The natural cycle of life goes on, plants grow. Lizzie can sit there in March and know by June there'll be a jungle of life, already having harvested broad beans ready to eat in her ideal feta and mint salad.

This continual growth and development is encouraging; that seedlings, then fruit appear gives Lizzie the reassurance and confidence that so too her ideas will grow and bear fruit.

And what's more she doesn't need a power socket or WiFi.

346 Care about where things come from and how they are made

One Saturday morning in July I waited for 20 minutes in the queue for coffee.

I could see the three women behind the bar were making coffee with great care and attention.

And nothing unusual in that.

But I wasn't in Soho or Shoreditch.

I was in the middle of a field in Suffolk, at the Latitude music festival, standing in line at the Greenpeace café.

I was struck by how much thought the women put into their craft for a bunch of strangers. The level of attention and detail was like you'd get for exacting regulars who have high levels of expectation. But this was for people they'd never see again. What did it matter to them? The baristas could have been half-hearted, sloppy, uncaring. But they weren't. It elevated the experience. Something as small as a cup of coffee.

Life is made up from these small experiences. So – whether it's the music I listen to, the coffee I drink or the food I buy – that's why I care about where things come from and how they are made.

347 Don't be for everybody

A couple of years ago a business school hired me to run a session.

From the moment they first hired me I was keen to point out that I might not be quite what they're looking for. I outlined what I was and what I wasn't.

I wear my red trainers, walk around the stage a lot and get excited, I told them. I sent them a video clip of me doing my signature session. I'm different – are you sure you want me? Yes, they said!

So I got on the plane. I ran my session.

Back in my hotel I phoned my wife.

'How did it go?'

'Yeah, really well,' I told her.

Ten days later the business school sent me the detailed feedback forms from every delegate. At the end of the form was a space where people could write their comments.

One wrote, 'This guy was really bad.'

Of course harsh feedback can be hard to take. But I've always known I wasn't for everybody. And that's okay.

348 Rise strong

In 2015, I was invited to speak at the Do Lectures. Standing on stage in an old barn in Wales, I opened up and told my real story for the first time. I talked about losing my way. I spoke about my struggles. It was the hardest talk I'd ever given.

A couple of months after returning from Wales, I started reading Brené Brown's book *Rising Strong*. Brené says she was raised to believe that vulnerability is a weakness. She's since discovered, however, that vulnerability is the best measure of your courage.

In order to 'rise strong', she says, you need to first own your story and be honest about the rubbish bits so that you can emerge with a new ending based on what you've learned along the way.

I found Brené's words powerful. Often in life it can feel uncomfortable to expose yourself, to be honest about what you are feeling and what you've gone through. But what I've learned, first on stage in an old barn and then in the pages of Brené's book, is how vulnerability is a strength, not a weakness.

349 Remember it's all a mess up close

I remember walking into a David Hockney exhibition at The Royal Academy. There were 83 portraits by him on the walls of the gallery. It was a magnificent body of work and I was totally taken by them, struck by the bold colours, the scale of the paintings, the sheer commitment on display.

When I leaned in, however, I spotted things I hadn't noticed from afar: crude strokes, imperfect fingers he'd painted, even white patches of canvas. My appreciation of the work didn't change one bit, I simply changed my perspective and stepped back again.

So while things look beautiful from one angle, close up things are quite different.

And I think that's important to remember. When you compare yourself with others, or when you always strive for perfection, what's perfect from a distance might be a mess up-close.

350 Shine a light on darkness

'How are you?'

I guess for years I would answer, 'Good thanks,' regardless of how I really felt. Perhaps many of us do that?

When my friend Jerry Colonna – who's an executive coach and founder of Reboot, a leadership and development firm – asks people how they are, he has a reputation for adding, 'No, I mean, *really*?' at the end.

Well it took me years to be open about how I was really feeling. To be comfortable talking about the struggles.

And what I learned is that when you shine a light on darkness, it becomes light. Acknowledging it and naming it makes a world of difference.

I recognize that my struggles have made me who I am.

So let's be more open about answering the 'How are you?' question. What I've discovered is that once you start to be honest, people around you have the confidence to share their own stories. They see it's okay to display their vulnerabilities.

So next time your friend asks how you are – do you think you can tell them how you really feel?

351 Build it on kindness

The world of work and business can feel cut-throat. Many of us have experienced work cultures where everyone is competing with each other, where egos clash and extroverts flourish.

I have visited hundreds of workspaces in my career.

And number 47 Bergen Street, Brooklyn stood out for being different.

It's the home of Friends Work Here, a co-working space founded by designer and creative entrepreneur Tina Roth Eisenberg.

It was a balmy spring day when I arrived at 47 Bergen Street. Outside the trees were in blossom. At first glance, the exposed brick and distressed wooden floors may have looked like your typical identikit co-work space found in any city around the world. But after a few minutes I could see this was special. There was a welcoming vibe as if you were visiting an apartment, not a workspace. It was intimate. Everyone was friendly. Tina told me Friends Work Here is a community built on kindness, no room for egos, everybody supporting each other, lifting each other up. How refreshing is that?

If surrounding yourself with kind, driven, creative people is your thing, you'll love it here, says the Friends Work Here website. Quick, grab a desk while you can.

352 Look in the rearview mirror

When you're right in the middle of it, sometimes it can be hard to identify the different chapters that make up your life journey. The conditions might be too foggy to spot the common thread or see your overarching purpose. But when you emerge on the other side you can take stock. Looking back in your rearview mirror will get you seeing clearly again, and help everything make sense. The rearview mirror will give you a sense of where you've come from, the hurdles and barriers you've had to overcome.

So when the journey gets tough, hang in there. Keep motoring forward. And once the fog lifts you'll have the clarity to help you better navigate the road ahead.

353 Make it better than it needs to be

A client asked if I could deliver the same presentation that I'd done for them last year.

Sure – I could've just recycled last year's slides and running order. But instead I spent time adding new elements, telling new stories, redesigning the slides. I had to make it better than it had been before, better than I wanted. Better than my client was expecting.

I once heard the writer Naomi Alderman talk about the creative process behind her running-based game 'Zombies, Run'. She explained her ethos is to make it better than it needs to be.

Making 'it' – your story, your workshop, your presentation, your report – better than it needs to be means you're increasing your chances of success.

If you only make it fit for purpose, someone might notice. And that someone is you. Throw everything into it and make it better than it needs to be.

354 Wear your red sneakers

A few years ago Professor Francesca Gino, author of *Rebel Talent*, decided to conduct an experiment in the executive education classes she was teaching at Harvard Business School.

With one group of students, she wore her dark blue Hugo Boss suit, a white silk blouse and dress shoes. For the next group, she slipped off her leather shoes and laced up a pair of red Converse sneakers.

There was a big difference between the two classes that day.

In the red-sneakers class the students were more attentive and thoughtful, and they laughed more. Part of the difference, she realized, was the effect the sneakers had on *her* – she felt more confident and more poised when leading discussions. At the end of the class, she gave out a short survey. The students rated her as having greater status when she wore the red shoes.

So what would you wear to bring yourself more confidence?

356 Lean into You

When do you feel most You?

As you read those six words I am sure you have a reaction to that question.

It might be easy to articulate or you may need to dig deeper but it's there.

When do I feel most Me? When I'm creating. Right now. Sitting at the bottom of my garden under a tree. Hitting the keys on my MacBook, writing these words, headphones in, listening to Arlo Parks.

Photography. Doodling as a school kid. Working in local radio as a teenager. Telling stories. Being on stage. Standing in the audience at a small, sweaty gig. Travelling around Europe by train.

There's a theme here. Experiences where I can be free, open, creative.

How about you? Dig deep – find the connection, or find the disparate elements – when you feel most You. Lean into it...

357 Throw a party for one

Depending on where you work you might have an annual party where you celebrate the year's achievements. There might be a speech by the boss, a nice dinner and awards for the staff.

But what happens if you don't work in a company and still want a party to celebrate? Terin Izil is a freelance creative director based in New York. When she hit her one year anniversary of working for herself she wanted to celebrate. So she threw herself a company party for one!

She gave out company awards, even delivered a state of the union address to herself. There was a takeaway lunch, a happy hour and a dinner cruise with a plus one!

She told me she had great fun!

(And if you want to organize your own Company Party of One, Terin has posted a checklist and templates on her website terindustries.net/companypartyofone)

358 Read for pleasure

I find it hard to switch off, but there's one thing I've realized in the last few years that consistently helps me to do just that: reading a novel. It doesn't have to be a work of literary genius, just something to get lost in. I've found that if I don't have a piece of fiction on the go, I'm not so relaxed and default to spending too much of the evening on my phone.

So whenever I start a new page-turner, I have that wonderful feeling again. Right now I've just finished *Fleishman Is in Trouble* by Taffy Brodesser-Akner and have picked up Delia Owens' *Where the Crawdads Sing*.

Novels transport me away every time. I really miss when I don't have one on the go. Need a recommendation? I've got a long list! And if you've got a page-turner to share, let me know!

359 Never use what you love as a stick to beat yourself with

I started following @ladyvelo on Instagram back in 2012 when I realized we shared a love of coffee shops. That started a longtime online friendship – we even managed to meet each other offline when I hosted an evening event with her in my hometown. She was there to talk about her book *Back in the Frame*.

Lady Vélo, a.k.a. Jools Walker, is an avid cyclist and blogger. In her book she writes about her passion for cycling and the part it plays in alleviating her depression. While she's passionate about cycling, she writes that getting back on her bike Frankie wasn't always a pleasure. Once, during a particularly difficult phase, the thought of cycling made her feel worse. She'd guilt herself into getting on her bike, and then realize the guilty feelings were another way for her to berate herself.

So when Jools was prescribed new medication, she took her time before working out a way to incorporate Frankie back into her day: she decided to cycle to work. Every day she altered the route to keep it fresh and she soon started to enjoy cycling again.

Jools is very much of the mindset that you have to do what's right for you, and never use what you love as a stick to beat yourself with, or when things don't quite go to plan.

360 Stay close to you

So we're nearly there. And at this point in your journey I want to remind you of something. To light this up in neon:

That the key to the meaning of life is this – knowing what is sacred, what really matters to you. Being in the now, celebrating being alive. Making the right choices that are aligned with your passions and values. Having agency where to put your attention. Identifying what freedom means to you and living by your rules, not someone else's. Being stimulated by a sense of purpose. Going with your gut.

Chuck all those things in and, for me, you get to the essence of what it means to live a good life.

CHAPTER 13
STICK TO WHO YOU ARE

361 Celebrate the glory – and the mess – of being human

As we near the final pages of the book, I want to make clear that tuning in to having more good days in your life is not about a happy-clappy 'everything is awesome' vibe. It's about recognizing who you are, your ups and your downs, and getting comfortable with that.

During the lockdown months of 2020, I had a wonderful couple of conversations with Jerry Colonna over in Boulder, Colorado. In a conversation we taped for my 'Meet The Storytellers' series (you can find it on YouTube) Jerry reminds us that life is a rollercoaster.

We are on a constant emotional ride.

First up, then down.

Up then down.

Up then down.

And despite what social media may tell you, no one's crushing it completely. No one is getting it right every single moment of every single day. And Jerry told me, when we pretend otherwise we make it really, really difficult for someone who's struggling. Because then the story they tell themselves is that I feel bad so I must be broken. But, says Jerry, here's the truth: you're not broken, you're just human, and with it comes all the glory and the mess that makes us who we are.

The glory. And the mess.

Amen to that.

362 Stick to who you are

Okay, the single most important thing I've learned in my life so far?

The one thing I'm going to make sure my kids remember, even when I'm not here anymore?

It's just nine words long:

> 'Stick to who you are and build on it.'

I believe so many of us would be happier – and more successful too – if only we could be better at being ourselves. Your true, deep, authentic self – before you got told you couldn't be something, or do something or express yourself how you want or need to.

Many of us have an understanding of who we are at an early age. You know what makes you tick, you know your strengths, what you love doing, what you stand for. If only you could use that sense of clarity as a foundation stone for the rest of your life.

So don't let teachers, careers advisors, bosses, partners, parents knock the You out of you. Stand back, discover who you are.

Stick to who you are and build on it.

363 What's your stop, start and amplify?

Exercise

During the dramatic changes of 2020, many of us had the chance for personal and professional reflection, thinking about how your life had changed and how you wanted to emerge from all this.

The world was full of advice.

But one post I saw on LinkedIn stuck with me. It asked a simple question in three parts: what's your stop, start and amplify?

Can you apply that right here, right now to redesigning your own life? Think about:

1. One thing you can stop doing.

2. One thing you'll start doing.

3. The behaviour, interest or element of you that you are going to amplify?!

364 Identify the one thing that's sacred to you

If you were going to narrow it down, what is the one ingredient that's sacred to having a good day?

Is it doing a daily doodle? A mid-morning mug of tea? A yoga session? Walking the dog? Ten minutes of meditation? Laughter? A human connection? A run?

Make it realistic and actionable.

Write it down. Pin it up. Hey get it tattooed on your wrist!

Make a daily commitment to it.

365 Chisel your manifesto in stone

It was a Monday morning in October 2012. Walking down Barcelona's Carrer d'Enric Granados I stumbled across Café Cosmo. It was busy and buzzy. I instantly felt at home there. As I sat with my espresso I got out my notepad and, without thinking, started a list. I headed it 'My Charter' and there and then quickly cranked out a list of twenty dos and don'ts.

I will play where I play best.

I will stay authentic to me and will not compromise.

I will continue to be driven by curiosity and will go out of my comfort zone to learn and develop.

Etc.

I hadn't planned to write it, but I suddenly got the focus and clarity to articulate what mattered most in my working life: I had accidentally created a manifesto.*

I think of a manifesto as a compass. It captures what you stand for, what makes you tick, what you will and won't do. It's like chiselling into stone your beliefs and values. It stands there strong and immutable, a guide to remind you who you are and which will help you navigate your paths and choices in life.

Write yours – take half an hour in your favourite armchair or coffee shop to write down your beliefs and values, your dos and don'ts.

Stick your manifesto up on the wall. Live by it.

The end

So there you go – those are my 365 ways to have a good day.

Every day is a chance to choose how you wish to be in the world. How you are with others. Where you put your attention. How you fill your body and your mind. Whether you're kind to yourself. What you take in. What you put out into the world.

So when you turn off the light tonight, will you be able to say 'yes, today I chose well'?

---

*Want to see mine from 2012? Email hello@iansanders.com and I will send it to you, along with my guide on how to write your own.

THANK YOU!

On the one hand I wrote this book quite fast – it was three months from being commissioned to delivering the manuscript. But the real story is that I've been working on this book for the last 10+ years. I wrote it slow, not fast.

In the 20 to 30 old notepads of mine that I mined for this project, lay the essence of this book. Those scribbles, observations and reflections from planes, trains and coffee shops – along with conversations with strangers, input from experts, insights from collaborators I've met and worked with – have informed the 365 ideas.

I'm really grateful to the following people for taking the time to share their reflections on having a good day and the ideas in this book:

Michael Acton Smith, Claire Atkinson, Sarah Barlow, Paul Benney, Michael Burne, Jerry Colonna, Nick Creswell, Sally Croft, Sam Dixon Brown, Sarah Ellis, Lizzie Everard, Sam Ford, Hugh Garry, Emma Gibbs De Oliveira, Bree Goff, Cali Harris, Dr Hazel Harrison, David Hieatt, Kelly Hoey, Terin Izil, Sarah King, Gillian Licari, Dr Peter Lovatt, Kevin Maguire, Emily Morris, Judi Oates, Sejal Parekh, Giles Pearman, Aimee Riordan, David Sloly, Matthew Stillman, Michael Townsend Williams, Helen Tupper, Claire Van der Zant, John Waire, Karen Wickre.

Thanks to all those people in organizations – from startups to global corporations – who have hired me over the years and provided that insight into what a good day at work looks like. From Amsterdam to Madrid, I've worked with some fascinating teams who've shone a light on the ingredients, habits and behaviours they need to have a good day.

And thanks to the hospitality of those coffee shop owners who have provided a space for me, my notepad and pencil over the years. From my home-town of Leigh-on-Sea to towns and cities across the globe, cafés and coffee shops have always provided a valuable space for me to do my best thinking and scribbling. Cheers for the fuel.

A special thanks to Zoë who's not only my wife, but also my creative partner. She's at my side on every project and this one was no exception. I really could not have produced this book without her support and ideas. In the final few weeks before I submitted the manuscript, her input was invaluable. She helped me wrangle the ideas into shape, told me which ones to ditch (harsh but necessary) and cast her editor eyes over every single idea before I handed it over to Iain and his team of experts at John Murray Learning. Thank you Zoë.

Thanks to Iain Campbell (so good to work together again!), Chloe West and Isabel Martin at John Murray Learning; to Sarah Orthmann and Melissa Carl at Nicholas Brealey Publishing; and to everyone else at Hachette who worked on the project.